GIVING
GOD
ULTIMATE
LOVE

GIVING
GOD
ULTIMATE
LOVE

OVER-THE-TOP MEGA LOVE

Bukky Agboola

CHORDS OF LOVE LLC

ISBN: 978-1-7335652-0-2 (Paperback Edition)
ISBN: 978-1-7335652-1-9 (Ebook / Kindle)
ISBN: 978-1-7335652-2-6 (Ebook / Epub)

Author cover image by Gina Gold, clouds by
Shutterstock © Deer worawut.
Edited by Mikel Benton
Book design by DesignforBooks.com

Printed in the United States of America.

Contents

Prologue

I pray this book will strengthen your faith in Jesus Christ
and transform your walk with God.
May you know Him more.
God bless you.

Dedication and Acknowledgments

To the Lord Jesus Christ,
Words are not enough to adore you for
Who you are and all that you have done.

My wonderful family,
Thank you for
Your loyal support and
Unwavering love.

Our powerful boutique church
(House of Prayer),
You're simply the best.

My publishing team,
Thank you for bringing these precious words to everyone.
You are a mega blessing.

Trust and Obey

When we walk with the Lord
In the light of His Word,
What a glory He sheds on our way!
While we do His good will,
He abides with us still,
And with all who will trust and obey.

Refrain:
Trust and obey,
For there's no other way
To be happy in Jesus,
But to trust and obey.

Not a shadow can rise,
Not a cloud in the skies,
But His smile quickly drives it away;
Not a doubt or a fear, not a sigh or a tear,
Can abide while we trust and obey.

Refrain:
Trust and obey,
For there's no other way
To be happy in Jesus,
But to trust and obey.

. . . .

Not a burden we bear,
Not a sorrow we share,
But our toil He doth richly repay;
Not a grief or a loss,
Not a frown or a cross,
But is blessed if we trust and obey.

Refrain:
Trust and obey,
For there's no other way
To be happy in Jesus,
But to trust and obey.

But we never can prove
The delights of His love
Until all on the altar we lay;
For the favor He shows,
And the joy He bestows,
Are for them who will trust and obey.

Refrain:
Trust and obey,
For there's no other way
To be happy in Jesus,
But to trust and obey.

Then in fellowship sweet
We will sit at His feet,
Or we'll walk by His side in the way;

What He says we will do,
Where He sends we will go;
Never fear, only trust and obey.

Refrain:
Trust and obey,
For there's no other way
To be happy in Jesus,
But to trust and obey.

—John H. Sammis, 1887.

1

Giving God
Ultimate Love!

A passionate praise dance to honor God ended a royal marriage, while one man's faithful obedience to Him would be viewed as attempted murder today and land him in jail. A devout woman's unrivalled trust in God was quite impressive, while another woman poured a $20,000 jar of perfume on Jesus just to show her love for God. By no means must we overlook the examples of a poor widow who surrendered her last two pennies to God with crazy faith and an extremely rich king who built Him a house of worship worth over $200 billion!

Also worth a mention is the faithful preacher who declared a midnight praise party for God after being almost beaten to death for preaching about Him. And then there is the example of some very wealthy men from the Middle East who left everything behind and journeyed for months just to worship God. So I guess the next thing to ask is, are you ready for this?

Human beings have what it takes to give God ultimate love.

The prophet Samuel's mother dedicated his life to God's service even before he was conceived (1 Sam. 1:9–11), and the selfless, low-key surrender of her life to God by Anna, a New Testament prophetess, also qualifies as giving God ultimate love. Many more examples of this amazing depth of love for God are found throughout the Bible, and each one of them is worthy of emulation.

These individuals gave God their over-the-top, mega love but, ultimately, Jesus Christ would leave us the perfect model for giving God ultimate love. Regardless of socioeconomic or any other status, and without holding anything back, people from all walks of life demonstrated their love for God in extraordinary ways. They leave us with life-changing lessons on trusting God and outstanding depictions of what it means to love God no matter what. Their over-the-top expressions of mega love were sometimes lavish, even outlandish, but one thing is for sure: ultimate is not average!

Receive the ultimate reward points! Get the ultimate restaurant freebies for your mum on Mother's Day! Get the ultimate Thanksgiving meal deal!

More ads like these to purchase the newest, fastest, and best are always on the rise, and companies will pull no punches to rally support for their newest products and services. We are subjected to too many advertising blitzes by companies seeking to increase their profit margins. Gimmicky advertising has become the new norm, and to gain an advantage over their competitors in an over-crowded market, the word *ultimate* often gets overused.

One of our popular fast-food chains claims it sells the *Ultimate Cheeseburger!* During the holidays there are plenty of offers to purchase from *The Ultimate Holiday Gift Guide. Get the ultimate release package!* was the title of an uninvited email I recently received in my inbox from a company I had previously done some business with, now offering me the opportunity to participate in their latest package deal. Our senses may be dulled to the meaning of *ultimate* and, as we are pressured to partici-pate in the latest offerings, our attitude might be, "I've seen and heard all of these before."

Manufacturers, service providers, and others rally sup-port for their wares or particular causes daily, and the mes-sage of highest standard for which *ultimate* ought to stand gets lost in the noise. The intended impact of this word has somewhat diminished, and we will need to remind ourselves of its true definition. *The Oxford English Dic-tionary* defines ultimate as "the best achievable or imagin-able of its kind," while the *Merriam-Webster Dictionary* describes it as "the best or most extreme of its kind: utmost."

Ultimate is meant to convey that whatever is being spoken of is the *ideal, greatest, supreme, unsurpassed, unrivalled, topmost, utmost, or just simply the best!*

In light of these definitions, have you ever given any thought to what you could give to God that would meet the standard for ultimate love? What would merit this term when it comes to loving God, and what springs to your mind when you first hear the words *ultimate love?* What is the greatest gift you can give to someone? The scriptures tell us, "Let love be your highest goal" (1 Cor. 14:1, New Living Translation).

Although the loud messaging has desensitized us to what we see and hear, we may need to change our attitudes from the negative, "I've seen and heard all of these before," to the more positive, "Be a people after God's own heart!" (Acts 13:22, NLT). The actions taken by the individuals mentioned earlier were as simple as a fervent display of praises to God or as opulent and lavish as the giving of extremely large and generous donations to His service. Some acts were privately done while others took place during corporate or public worship.

Learning how to love God the mega, over-the-top way will require that we dive into the scriptures to uncover what God's viewpoint on our theme is, and the hunt for the truth on any given subject must begin with the Bible. When we understand the Bible correctly, God's wisdom is revealed to us, and His Holy Spirit assists us in arriving at the correct conclusions.

All Scripture is inspired by God and is useful to teach us what is true and to make us realize what is wrong in our lives. It corrects us when we are wrong and teaches us to do what is right" (2 Tim. 3:16, NLT).

Then Jesus asked them, "Didn't you ever read this in the Scriptures?" (Matt. 21:42, NLT).

For everything that was written in the past was written to teach us (Rom. 15:4, New International Version).

Our mission is not a pie-in-the-sky dream. When we approach the word of God not as theologians or experts, but as true lovers of God seeking our heavenly Father's heart, anyone desiring to go after God fervently can do so. Absolute trust in the veracity and integrity of God's word, combined with a sincere hunger for the truth, will help us to reach the proper understanding. The Holy Spirit guides us in finding the truth, and our focus must be on the scriptures.

When the Spirit of truth comes, He will guide you into all truth. He will not speak on his own but will tell you what he has heard (John 16:13, NLT).

The Bible also tells us that when we ask God for anything, if we believe, we will receive answers to our

questions. This may include questions about God Himself. We may not always get the answers we want, but we
are assured of a response to our requests. If we have faith,
God has promised that anyone who draws closer to Him
will be richly rewarded. Those who delight themselves
in God receive the desires of their heart from Him. Our
faith in God pleases Him, and the goal of our quest is to
freshly determine how to adore and esteem God at the
highest level.

Can we love God this way?

> If you believe, you will receive whatever you ask
> for in prayer (Matt. 21:22, NIV).

> Delight yourself in the LORD, and he will give
> you the desires of your heart (Ps. 37:4, English
> Standard Version).

> Come close to God, and God will come close
> to you (James 4:8, NLT).

> And without faith it is impossible to please
> God, because anyone who comes to him must
> believe that he exists and that he rewards those
> who earnestly seek him (Heb. 11:6, NIV).

Let's start by taking a look at the Bible's definition of
love. We will then move on to discover what unsurpassable

love for the Lord is. The ancient Greek language of the Bible used four different words to describe love. They are *eros*, *philia*, *storge*, and *agape*.

The word *eros* describes the romantic physical attraction and intimacy that takes place between a man and woman. This form of love should be strictly reserved for marriage and was given by God for married couples to bond at the highest emotional, physical, and spiritual levels. When the two take exclusive pleasure in one another's bodies, they experience *eros* and stay attached at the ultimate level. Sharing this closest of ties makes the two become one, helping them to stay devoted to one another for a lifetime. This makes their union complete.

Although eros is not used in the New Testament, it is clearly illustrated in the Old Testament book of The Song of Solomon. And we also see it at work in all the love stories in the Bible. Abraham and Sarah, Jacob and Rachel, Ruth and Boaz are all illustrations of the enduring love that can develop between a man and woman, and this creates the foundation for the family.

The next type of love is known as *storge*. This word describes the type of love found in families. It is the bond between mothers, fathers, sons and daughters, sisters and brothers. *Storge* is not used in the New Testament, but its opposite form *astorgos*, meaning heartless, unfeeling, or without family love, is used in Romans 1:31 and 2 Timothy 3:3.

The word *astorgos* describes people without affection for their families or relatives, and the absence of *storge* or the presence of *astorgos* in our world is another unhappy indicator that we are living in the end times, a sad reminder of the wickedness that will be prevalent during the days before the second coming of Jesus Christ.

The highest of these four types of love is *agape*. It is the selfless, sacrificial, and unconditional love that best describes God's love for human beings. God's inexhaustible love is always at work to restore humankind. God fully demonstrated His love by His willingness to sacrifice His only Son on the cross to pay for all our sins. God made the ultimate sacrifice when He did this, and although the subject of love evokes many images, God's love is unequalled. We are able to understand only a little in comparison to the greatness of His love.

Jesus revealed God's agape love for human beings when He paid the full penalty for our sins on the cross.

The full pardon that comes freely to human beings cost God everything. If we desire to give God ultimate love, we will first need to experience His agape love. The strength of God's love cannot be compared to frail human love, and God is the only one worthy of receiving our ultimate love. Agape love is so sweet that it ought to restore our self-worth and fill our hearts with delight that this is the type of love that God has for us.

I delight greatly in the LORD; my soul rejoices in my God. For he has clothed me with garments of salvation and arrayed me in a robe of his righteousness (Isa. 61:10, NIV).

For God loved the world so much that he gave his one and only Son, so that everyone who believes in him will not perish but have eternal life (John 3:16, NLT).

For the Father himself loves you dearly because you love me and believe that I came from God (John 16:27, NLT).

The next word used to describe love in the Bible is *philia.* This type of love best describes the close friendships or brotherly love among human beings. The word for this kind of love is the most commonly used one in the Bible and includes within its definition the compassion we ought to have for one another, especially those in need among us.

God has set the example of ultimate love for us to follow, and our willingness to love and forgive one another ought to spring from the knowledge that God so dearly loves us. His love enables us to become a part of His love resources on the earth, and as we share God's love with one another, our world will become a far better place to live.

Let us love one another, for love comes from
God. Everyone who loves has been born of God
and knows God. Whoever does not love does
not know God, because God is love. If someone
says, "I love God," but hates a Christian brother
or sister, that person is a liar; for if we don't love
people we can see, how can we love God, whom
we cannot see? And he has given us this command: Those who love God must also love their
Christian brothers and sisters (1 John 4:7–8,
20–21, NIV).

By this all people will know that you are my
disciples, if you have love for one another (John
13:35, ESV).

By this we know love that he laid down his life
for us, and we ought to lay down our lives for
the brothers (1 John 3:16, ESV).

Our acts of service toward God and our fellow men
are ways to show our love for Him. They are special
expressions of love that give us the privilege of partner-
ing with God in His great work of restoration on our
planet. We become God's ambassadors on the earth and
a vital part of this plan. People who love God and those
He has placed in their lives are the living, breathing,
moving, holy dwelling places through whom God can

bring about His will and purposes on the earth. When the good news of God's love is shared with others, the knowledge of it will become so widely known that His amazing grace will be experienced by everyone.

Will you let your roots grow deep down into God's love, producing a mighty harvest of over-the-top, mega love for Him that transforms our world?

2

Finding True Love in a Broken World

Let's talk a little more about love. How does the world see it, and what more can we understand about it? The secular world defines *love* as "an intense feeling or very deep affection for a person."

It is also defined as "tenderness, fondness, adoration, worship, or devotion."

The emotion of love, although hard to describe, brings much delight to people's hearts. It can be quite amusing when a person gets drunk on love. They say and do things both privately and publicly that they would normally not have the nerve to do, and they may go around singing, *"I'm in love, I'm in love, I'm in love!"* Have you ever been with or seen someone in love? They go completely "gaga" (for want of a better word) over the one whom they love. We've all heard about butterflies in the stomach, the day-dreaming about the loved one, or just simply gazing at the loved one's picture. You don't have to admit this to me—and I'm not saying I did this—but have you ever called a loved one's phone number, knowing he can't pick up, just to hear his voice on the voicemail message? If you do this, you may be in love. We just can't get enough of the person we're in love with and can't get him out of our heads! We get giddy with excitement at the mere mention of his name and believe that he is special, focusing mostly on his positive qualities.

You can fill in the gaps with your own experiences and stories of being in love. Love can be between family members—husband and wife, mother and son or daughter, father and son or daughter, and so on. Imagine the absolute thrill of a devoted spouse excitedly waiting for a loved one to step off an airplane after a safe return home from military service, or the joyful anticipation of a mom or dad expecting a son or daughter back home from an out-of-state college. We always want to be close with the ones whom we love, and we devote ourselves entirely to pleasing them. When we love someone, we become more willing to participate in activities that were previously outside our usual range if they are of interest to our loved one, such as bowling, dancing, shopping, new foods, changing the way we dress or do our hair, and so on.

We want to spend lots of time with the ones we love and, if practical, would spend most of our time with them. People give up great wealth, powerful positions, and extremely rare and precious treasures to secure the love of their fellow humans. We may have read stories about people who gave up great inheritances just to be with the ones they loved, and many books, songs, movies, and television dramas compete daily to depict what love is. Bestsellers have been written about the topic, and artists and writers compete with one another to depict love and tell us great love stories.

The presence or absence of this emotion is used to justify actions taken or not taken by main characters in their many love stories, and the resources to tell us more about love only keep growing. Artists and writers attempt to convey their viewpoints on this captivating subject, and human beings' obsession with love makes it arguably the world's most engaging topic. Many talk-show hosts capitalize on the passion that love stimulates to gain higher ratings, and the great lengths to which people will go to win someone's heart is quite fascinating.

Love also makes us more sensitive to another person's pain. We are willing to make great sacrifices for the ones whom we love, but of course the opposite rings true when we fall out of love. There are many tragic stories of the sad outcomes of unrequited love or the end or failure of love. Some people lose their dignity and composure temporarily while trying desperately to hold on to what they have determined is true love, while others may become overly possessive and irrationally jealous over the ones whom they love. The feeling of lingering loneliness left in people's hearts when love comes to an end can also be palpable, and the results of losing a loved one can be heartbreaking. Human beings' use of trial and error to obtain, maintain, and retain love is right at the heart of our topic. It begets this question: To whom should we be so devoted?

People's attempts to find and hold on to love indicate that there is a lack of understanding about its true origins. The origin and source of love is God.

"God is love" (1 John 4:8, NIV). It is in Him that true love is found. We all want to be held dear in someone's heart, and the intense cravings we all have for love are an outward manifestation of a much deeper pining, the longing for God.

Frail and temporal human love can never satisfy our need for love. It may, in fact, lead us into greater disappointment. Fulfillment and genuine happiness occur when we connect ourselves with God and His love. He is the primary originator of it, and the scriptures tell us that love does not begin with human beings but comes directly from God.

> Love comes from God. Everyone who loves has been born of God and knows God (1 John 4:7, NIV).

> We know how much God loves us, and we have put our trust in his love. God is love, and all who live in love live in God, and God lives in them (1 John 4:16, NLT).

In our broken and hurting world, human beings made in the image of a loving God will spend a lifetime trying to locate and hold on to love. This is an attempt to satisfy the deepest longing within us, the desire for God's eternal love. His *agape* love has been fully revealed through Jesus Christ, and the onus is on us to receive God's love. When we recognize the great lengths to which God has gone to rescue His lost children from the powers of darkness, we must acknowledge that we are dearly loved and greatly cherished by Him. Our decision to receive the free pardon God offers and fully embrace His grace instantly restores us into His family. To experience real contentment in our lives, we first need to be captivated by God's love.

God's love delivered us from the powers of sin and the grave. We must therefore seek ways to express our utmost love for Him.

We rediscover our true value through God's eyes and the tremendous sacrifice He made to save human beings. *Agape* love is beyond description. Thanksgiving, praise, and adoration ought to flow easily from our hearts toward God daily as the right response to His ultimate love. The desperate, committed, and passionate heart of God is always at work to recover His lost children, and before it becomes too late, we must humble ourselves and receive His free gift of salvation and eternal life. God's love is unsurpassable; establishing a right relationship with Him is the foundation for true love.

This is real love—not that we loved God, but
that he loved us and sent his Son as a sacrifice
to take away our sins (1 John 4:10, NLT).

Jesus also wants his followers to love God and one
another. But we cannot give to others what we do not
possess. Until we are reconnected back to the source of
love, we are unable to genuinely love one another sincerely in the long term, because only great lovers of God
can be great lovers of people.

Let all that you do be done in love (1 Cor.
16:14, ESV).

We all feel longings for love on the inside because
we are created in the image and likeness of a loving God.
Our dream of being unconditionally loved will be truly
fulfilled only when we come back into a right relationship with Him. God is the true source of love, and our
hearts desperately need His love. When we connect with
Him, we receive the grace that enables us to love others
and gives us the power to live victorious lives.

Anyone—regardless of ethnicity, gender, or status—
can repent of his or her sins and accept Jesus Christ as
his or her Savior. He has made the payment for all our
past, present, and future wrongdoings. The key to finding
true love is to restore our broken relationship with God.

Greater love has no one than this: to lay down one's life for one's friends (John 15:13, NIV).

Although we were unworthy and may never love Him back, Jesus was still willing to die to protect those whom He loved.

God's *agape* love is the only form of love that can truly satisfy our soul's needs and is the foundation for abundant living. It is the cure-all for all our lovesickness. Although the word *love* has lost some of its original depth because of our overuse, it is still the most beautiful word in the world. Without meaning to do so, we may have diminished its impact by the way we express fondness for and attachment to people and things: *"I love my family," "I love my friends," "I love my new shoes," "I love my favorite designer clothing,"* or *"I love my favorite food."*

We also love our cars, music, sports, favorite celebrities, video games, and so on. We love a whole bunch of stuff! While it is healthy to express our affection for people and some things, the overuse of *love* may dilute the fullest sense of its message. Our use of the word *love* verges on trivialization, and we might need to recapture the fullness of this most important word. To give God ultimate love, we must first understand that He is the source of love. Restoring Him to the rightful first place in our hearts means that we've finally located true love. The most impressive love story is that of God's love for human beings. We are reminded in the Bible that our value in God's eyes far outweighs all the gold, silver, diamonds, rubies, or other things of great value that this world has to offer.

The ransom for a life is costly, no payment is ever enough (Ps. 49:8, NIV).

And what do you benefit if you gain the whole world but lose your own soul? Is anything worth more than your soul? (Mark 8:36, NLT).

The fulfilment we seek for our hearts is found only in God; His relentless passion to win us back cannot be matched by any form of human love. God revealed the worth of a human soul by the unquantifiable price He was willing to pay for it. I must add that although aspiring to give God ultimate love is highly commendable, we are not trying to place any heavy burdens upon ourselves. It might seem impossible to expect imperfect human beings to give their perfect Creator the utmost in any way. But although our aspiration sounds daunting, let's be determined to take up the gauntlet for this most worthy of causes and allow the scriptures to guide us to what we can genuinely offer to God that can merit the term *ultimate love.*

How will you demonstrate your love to God? Is He the ultimate love of your life?

3

Why Did God Create People?

To make further advances in our quest to give God ultimate love, we need to ask another important question. *Why did God create people?* What was His motive for creating our planet and all the beautiful things on it? Also, what went wrong? Why do we experience destruction, chaos, and pain instead of God's love? Again, our answers are found in the scriptures. From them we learn that God is the first cause of everything.

People were originally created by God to be His family forever, and He's never going to change His mind about this.

He created our beautiful planet and all the wonderful things on it as a perfect dwelling place for the human beings He dearly loved.

You alone are the LORD. You made the heavens, even the highest heavens, and all their starry host, the earth and all that is on it, the seas and all that is in them. You give life to everything, and the multitudes of heaven worship you (Nehemiah 9:6, NIV).

This is what the Lord Almighty, the God of Israel, says: "Tell this to your masters: With my great power and outstretched arm I made the earth and its people and the animals that are on it, and I give it to anyone I please" (Jer. 27:4–5, NIV).

For in Him all things were created, things in heaven and on earth, visible and invisible, whether thrones or dominions or rulers or authorities. All things were created through Him and for Him. He is before all things, and in Him all things hold together (Col. 1:16–17, Berean Study Bible).

"You are worthy, O Lord our God, to receive glory and honor and power. For you created all things, and they exist because you created what you pleased" (Revelation 4:11, NLT).

After creating the animals to provide companionship for human beings, God formed the first two human beings from the dust of the earth and breathed His life into them. He created both the male and female, and the book of Genesis records the creation of human beings as follows:

> Then the LORD God formed man of dust from the ground, and breathed into his nostrils the breath of life; and man became a living being. The Lord God planted a garden in Eden in the east, and there he placed the man he had made (Gen. 2:7–8, NLT).

> God created man in His own image, in the image of God He created him; male and female He created them (Gen. 1:27, New American Standard Bible).

After His awe-inspiring creation was completed, God placed the first two human beings in a beautiful garden planted especially for them with His own hands. God initiated the love relationship between Himself and human beings. We were created and destined by God to be an eternal part of divinity—what an amazing start! Human beings inherited all that God had made and were predestined to be His very own kin. We did absolutely *nothing* to create or deserve all that we now possess. In His unfathomable love, God created people in His own image to be the earthly part of His eternal family. He loved us first. All we ever did was show up! And all that God ever desired was to be our loving parent.

> I thought to myself, "I would love to treat you as my own children! I wanted nothing more than to give you this beautiful land—the finest possession in the world. I looked forward to your calling me 'Father,' and I wanted you never to turn from me" (Jer. 3:19, NLT).

None of the extraordinary events of creation happened because of any human decision or know-how. We did not come into existence of our own free will, nor do we know exactly how God formed us from the dust of the earth.

We also cannot fully comprehend the depths of God's amazing love. Human beings are simply the recipients of the wonderful gift of life. God is the alpha and omega (beginning and end), and our lives begin and conclude with Him.

Out of His immense love, God came up with the idea of having human beings in His divine family.

The generous act of creation, along with our heavenly Father's love and protection and all the provision humankind could ever need, ought to be more than enough of a reason to show gratitude to God and give Him our ultimate love. Human beings were given everything they could ever desire, and God's magnanimity was full proof of how much He dearly loved them. The first two human beings were also entrusted with all the power anyone could ever desire. Adam and Eve were given complete dominion over all the earth. God made us the masterpiece of His creation and masters of our planet: "For we are God's masterpiece. He has created us anew in Christ Jesus, so we can do the good things he planned for us long ago" (Eph. 2:10, NIV).

They also had total control over the other creatures God had made with a clear mandate to subdue, be productive, and take full charge of their new environment. "God blessed them; and God said to them, 'Be fruitful and multiply, and fill the earth, and subdue it; and rule over the fish of the sea and over the birds of the sky and over every living thing that moves on the earth'" (Gen. 1:28, NASB).

After providing them with the ideal environment in which they could live and thrive, God instructed them how they could successfully occupy and manage their new habitat. As proof that His original intent was for human beings to live forever, God forbade them from ever eating the fruit from the only tree in the garden that could bring about their demise, the tree of the knowledge of good and evil. To further affirm that His original intention was for them to never die; they could freely eat from the fruit of the *tree of life* and every other tree in the garden.

Out of the ground the LORD God caused to grow every tree that is pleasing to the sight and good for food; the tree of life also in the midst of the garden, and the tree of the knowledge of good and evil . . . . Then the LORD God took the man and put him into the garden of Eden to cultivate it and keep it. The LORD God commanded the man, saying, "From any tree of the garden you may eat freely. But from the tree of the knowledge of good and evil you shall not eat, for in the day that you eat from it you will surely die" (Gen. 2:9, 15–17, NASB).

"It's only the fruit from the tree in the middle of the garden that we are not allowed to eat. God said, 'You must not eat it or even touch it; if you do, you will die'" (Gen. 3:3, NLT).

God made it abundantly clear that death was never a part of His plan for humanity, and eternal life was granted to human beings from the start. Our true origins are rooted in God's love. Eternal love gave us eternal life. We received the most immense gifts that could ever be given—our lives and an entire planet! The idyllic life God originally blessed human beings with was filled with love, companionship, and a great potential for future prosperity for their offspring. Living in such close union with their Creator and enjoying the fellowship of one another, human beings had it made. They had been blessed with the perfect life. After completing His great work of creation, God rested on the seventh day and visited His new family regularly in their beautiful new garden.

The first two human beings freely received all these immense blessings and advantages. All that was required of them was to obey God's instructions completely. He was their great benefactor and the source of all that they had. He was also the only one with a perfect understanding of how everything He had created works.

God created human beings to be His family forever. His original intent cannot be improved upon.

It was not too much for God to expect human beings to be faithful stewards of all they had been given after they received His gift of life and more benefits than anyone could ever ask for. Human beings should have trusted and fully obeyed their Creator, considering the enormous blessings and great power He had freely bestowed on them. His love and trustworthiness had been clearly proven, and they only needed to be good stewards of what they had received. Had they chosen to do this, all would have been well with them and their posterity. But instead of returning God's love, the first two human beings responded with incomprehensible distrust.

Now the serpent was more crafty than any beast of the field which the LORD God had made. And he said to the woman, "Indeed, has God said, you shall not eat from any tree of the garden?" The woman said to the serpent, "From the fruit of the trees of the garden we may eat; but from the fruit of the tree which is in the middle of the garden, God has said, 'You shall not eat from it or touch it, or you will die. The serpent said to the woman, "You surely will not die! For God knows that in the day you eat from it your eyes will be opened, and you will be like God, knowing good and evil." When the woman saw that the tree was good for food, and that it was a delight to the eyes, and that the tree was desirable to make one wise, she took from its fruit and ate; and she gave also to her husband with her, and he ate. Then the eyes of both of them were opened, and they knew that they were naked; and they sewed fig leaves together and made themselves loin coverings (Gen. 3:1–7, NASB).

The enemy of all that was good had sneaked into their garden and successfully tempted human beings, causing them to fall away completely from God. Instead of giving love back to God, human beings committed the ultimate treason for no good reason, disobeying the only directive God had given them. Sadly, their treason would lead immediately to the complete downfall of humankind.

Through this one awful act, Adam and Eve committed the original sin, and their sin would wreak destruction on all creation. God had left them fully in charge,
but by following the serpent's words rather than God's
instructions, they had rebelled against God and violated
the trust placed in them. Their idyllic lifestyle was suddenly interrupted by evil, and after this encounter with
Satan, their idyllic relationship with God was completely destroyed. Adam and Eve demonstrated disloy-
alty and disobedience toward God and thereby lost their
immortality and all that they had been blessed with. This
extremely sad event in human history caused all human
beings to lose the gift of eternal life. They lost everything
they had received, and their direct access to God was also
completely lost. Everything bestowed on them was gone,
and instead of flourishing forever, human beings would
now meet evil head-on but would not be able to prevent
it. Had they simply obeyed God's instructions, everyone
to come after them would have also continued to enjoy
all these awesome God-given privileges.

Human beings would now experience hell on
earth as their new lot in life, with no power to overcome it. They would face overwhelming adversities in
every respect, with no escape from the effects of their
wickedness and great disobedience. In this immature
state, Adam and Eve could not have envisioned the
level of destruction they had brought upon themselves
and the entire planet. Sadness, disasters, never-ending

tragedies, unquantifiable suffering, and ultimately
death became the new lot of human beings. Because of
their sin against God, many previously unknown things
would enter the earth.

Human life was permanently and seemingly irreversibly altered. In their new place in life, everything
we dread became reality as colossal destruction came to
the earth. God's response to their treachery had to be
swift and drastic. His judgement and punishment were
promptly issued in comparable levels to the revelation
of His person and love they had been privileged to have.
Everyone involved in this great fiasco had to take responsibility for his own individual contribution.

> Then the Lord God said to the serpent, "Because
> you have done this, you are cursed more than all
> animals, domestic and wild. You will crawl on
> your belly, groveling in the dust as long as you
> live. And I will cause hostility between you and
> the woman, and between your offspring and her
> offspring. He will strike your head, and you will
> strike his heel." Then he said to the woman, "I
> will sharpen the pain of your pregnancy, and
> in pain you will give birth. And you will desire
> to control your husband, but he will rule over
> you. And to the man he said, "Since you lis-
> tened to your wife and ate from the tree whose
> fruit I commanded you not to eat, the ground

is cursed because of you. All your life you will struggle to scratch a living from it. It will grow thorns and thistles for you, though you will eat of its grains. By the sweat of your brow will you have food to eat until you return to the ground from which you were made. For you were made from dust, and to dust you will return" (Gen. 3:14–19, NASB).

Therefore the Lord God sent him out from the garden of Eden, to cultivate the ground from which he was taken. He drove the man out; and at the east of the garden of Eden he stationed the cherubim and the flaming sword which turned every direction to guard the way to the tree of life (Gen. 23–24, ESV).

Spiritually, physically, morally, and in every other way they were broken. They were ordered to leave their beautiful garden to restart life without God in the dark unknown. This must have been one of the saddest days for our Creator, the day He seemingly lost His human family forever. The only day that would far surpass this one in the level of pain God would have to endure was when He had to offer up His only Son to redeem human beings from their devastating fall.

But all praises be to God! In the midst of the awful devastation, God did not give up on human beings.

He would proceed to give all of creation the greatest lesson on love ever known. God chose to deliver human beings from their predicament and, by so doing, preserved creation from eternal doom. He took upon Himself the full responsibility for their sin against Him, and after punishing all the participants in the gigantic mess, He began to make a new way out for human beings. After the masterpiece of His creation betrayed Him, God responded with extravagant love. His loving response far surpassed anything anyone could have imagined. He began with offering Adam and Eve immediate forgiveness. The stated punishment for their sins was death, but God immediately substituted the blood of sinless animals for their sins.

> But you must not eat from the tree of the knowledge of good and evil, for when you eat from it you will certainly die (Gen. 2:17, NIV).

> For the wages of sin is death, but the free gift of God is eternal life through Christ Jesus our Lord (Rom. 6:23, NLT).

> "And the Lord God made clothing from animal skins for Adam and his wife" (Gen. 3:21, NIV).

By using the blood of innocent animals as a substitute, God could prevent their instant and eternal demise until the time when the perfect sacrifice of His son Jesus Christ would completely take away all sins. This was the only way God could temporarily cover their sins, and Adam and Eve were still very much loved by God. After enforcing all the consequences and punishment for their wrongdoings, God continued the enormous task of rescuing them and restoring creation. He began to create a new way to rescue human beings from eternal death, and although they had to be punished, their loving heavenly parent did not stop taking care of them.

> Even before he made the world, God loved us and chose us in Christ to be holy and without fault in his eyes. God decided in advance to adopt us into his own family by bringing us to himself through Jesus Christ. This is what he wanted to do, and it gave him great pleasure (Eph. 1:4–5, NLT).

> The Lamb who was slain from the creation of the world (Rev. 13:8, NIV).

This explains why God deserves our utmost love. We must show our love to the God of love. It is also wise for us to commit completely to obeying God. We must remember that our lives are a gift from Him. To enjoy the rich, satisfying life God has in mind for human beings, we must immediately repent of our sins and yield ourselves completely to His instructions. Had Adam and Eve trusted the one who was responsible for their lives and blessings, they would have avoided their great catastrophe. Instead, their disobedience triggered the worst disaster ever, the full magnitude of which they could comprehend only after the fact. This unfortunate turn of events could only be turned around by God. We learn from all these events that strict adherence to God's word is vital to our lives. Our need to trust God and carefully obey His commands will not change.

> God's commandments are critical to our existence. The key to a successful life is found only in them: "Take hold of my instructions; don't let them go. Guard them, for they are the key to life" (Prov. 4:13, NLT).

Ultimately, Jesus Christ would be the bridge to reconnect us to God. To paraphrase Eugene O'Neill, creation is broken, God is mending, and grace is the glue. Giving God our ultimate love ought to be our joyful human response to His great love. God took the full responsibility for our sins against Him and sent His sinless Son to pay the complete price for all our wrongdoings. Until Jesus could come to permanently take away all sin, pain, suffering, and death would rule supreme on the earth.

After Adam and Eve's disobedience, human beings no longer enjoyed automatic access to God, and everything would have been lost forever if not for God's grace. He provided a new way for us to rejoin His awesome eternal family. By this new method, we are able to enjoy again the close union we once had with God, and because of His tremendous sacrifice we are saved. It behooves us to take full advantage of and reciprocate God's wonderful love.

Adam and Eve did not realize how much God loved them till they lost everything. Do we?

4

Ultimate Grace
Deserves Ultimate Love

After ultimate evil successfully attacked God's dream of having human beings in His family forever, He did not take things lying down! As far as God was concerned, any attack against His children was an attack against Him. God began his steps to recover His lost family with a countermeasure against Satan. As we already learned, God had developed a plan to deal with human beings' original sin and made special garments of animal skins to cover their nakedness. God still loved human beings and was not going to give up on His dream of having us in His family forever. He unleashed His amazing grace, turned against Satan, and would ultimately destroy the forces of evil that took His children captive in order to rescue us.

God is the original and ultimate superhero in my eyes. God chose to exercise ultimate forgiveness and, by so doing, kept His family together.

The many steps God implemented to make it possible for humankind to come back to Him would ultimately culminate in the death of His only begotten Son. Under the new order of things, the lives of the fallen human beings would be completely different, no longer idyllic. God had shown them mercy by not destroying the first two human beings and relegating them to the scrap heap. This would have been the simplest and least painful option for God to take. He could simply have destroyed Adam and Eve before they began to multiply and made an entirely new type of creature for Himself. But when human beings fell from grace, the scriptures tell us that God showed the depths of His amazing grace by doing this instead:

> When we were utterly helpless, Christ came at just the right time and died for us sinners. Now, most people would not be willing to die for an upright person, though someone might perhaps be willing to die for a person who is especially good. But God showed his great love for us by sending Christ to die for us while we were still sinners. And since we have been made right in God's sight by the blood of Christ, he will certainly save us from God's condemnation. For since our friendship with God was restored by the death of his Son while we were still his enemies, we will certainly be saved through the life

of his Son. So now we can rejoice in our wonderful new relationship with God because our Lord Jesus Christ has made us friends of God. When Adam sinned, sin entered the world. Adam's sin brought death, so death spread to everyone, for everyone sinned. . . . But there is a great difference between Adam's sin and God's gracious gift. For the sin of this one man, Adam, brought death to many. But even greater is God's wonderful grace and his gift of forgiveness to many through this other man, Jesus Christ. And the result of God's gracious gift is very different from the result of that one man's sin. For Adam's sin led to condemnation, but God's free gift leads to our being made right with God, even though we are guilty of many sins. For the sin of this one man, Adam, caused death to rule over many. But even greater is God's wonderful grace and his gift of righteousness, for all who receive it will live in triumph over sin and death through this one man, Jesus Christ. Yes, Adam's one sin brings condemnation for everyone, but Christ's one act of righteousness brings a right relationship with God and new life for everyone" (Rom. 5:6–12, 15–18, NLT).

He had made a completely new way to reconnect human beings to His family. But because Adam and Eve had chosen to obey the serpent instead of God, they now had a new satanic nature and not their previous godly nature. They could no longer consistently walk in love with God and one another, and human beings in their fallen state possessed the knowledge of good and evil.

The evil they practiced gave rise to many atrocities on the earth. In place of the one commandment they had received from God, they now needed many new laws to regulate their fallen and satanic nature so that human life and families could continue in a somewhat civil manner on our planet. God had to give fallen humanity new rules for living and loving. They had no way of escaping the hell that they had released upon themselves and desperately needed fresh guidance from their Creator. But although Adam and Eve had brought indescribable doom upon all creation, God would not forsake them.

In all that would unfold, we can learn irreplaceable lessons about our union with God. God is faithful, and He stands by His word. The words "God is love" would now take on breathtaking dimensions! God's limitless capacity to forgive was put on full display. He took upon Himself the suffering for our sins through the arduous, excruciating death on a cross of His only Son, for that was the only way God could permanently pay for and eternally erase our sins.

The correction of our fatal error would cost God everything. A love that can endure utter and fatal failure is, indeed, true love.

Jesus Christ is the greatest manifestation of God's ultimate love. God made a way for us to come out of the enormous mess we had made and again be included in His eternal family. God's original dream drove His Son to the cross. Gratitude, humility, adoration, and love are the appropriate responses for humankind toward such a loving and compassionate God. And this would still be inadequate reciprocation for His great love. He will never alter His mind on His promise to love and care us, and the immense task of restoring creation to His original plan still continues today.

For God so loved the world that he gave his one and only Son, that whoever believes in him shall not perish but have eternal life (John 3:16, (NIV).

He who did not spare His own Son but gave Him up for us all (Rom. 8:32, BSB).

He is so rich in kindness and grace that he purchased our freedom with the blood of his Son and forgave our sins (Eph. 1:7, NLT).

For everyone has sinned; we all fall short of
God's glorious standard. Yet God, with unde-
served kindness, declares that we are righteous.
He did this through Christ Jesus when he freed
us from the penalty for our sins. For God presented Jesus as the sacrifice for sin. People are
made right with God when they believe that
Jesus sacrificed his life, shedding his blood. This
sacrifice shows that God was being fair when
he held back and did not punish those who
sinned in times past (Rom. 3:23–25, NLT).

But God showed his great love for us by sending Christ to die for us while we were still sinners . . . . So just as sin ruled over all people and
brought them to death, now God's wonderful
grace rules instead, giving us right standing
with God and resulting in eternal life through
Jesus Christ our Lord (Rom. 5:1, 8, NLT).

God's plan to rescue human beings was completed
when He sacrificed His only Son. "Jesus said, 'It is finished'" (John 19:30, NIV). His love is incomprehensible
and unfathomable. Although we had lost our original
access to Him at the fall, God's mercy still flowed toward
us like a river through Jesus Christ. Let us embrace
God's ultimate grace in all our ways and acknowledge
that God's love is far superior to human love.

So God can point to us in all future ages as examples of the incredible wealth of his grace and kindness toward us, as shown in all he has done for us who are united with Christ Jesus. God saved you by his grace when you believed. And you can't take credit for this; it is a gift from God (Eph. 2:7–8, NLT).

God is the consummate lover. The great lengths to which He is willing to go to save His lost children from eternal destruction ought to motivate us to give Him our ultimate love. He continues to stretch out His merciful hands and beckons each one of us to return to Him. The recipients of such great love ought to show their appreciation by asking for His forgiveness for their own sins and accepting Jesus Christ as their Savior. His sacrifice pays for all of our sins, and God's free and complete pardon restores us fully to His family. Jesus is our way-maker. Repenting from sin and demonstrating gratitude toward God is the beginning of our complete restoration.

Love does not delight in evil but rejoices with the truth. It always protects, always trusts, always hopes, and always perseveres. Love never fails (1 Cor. 13:6–8, NIV).

God's gift of a total release from all past, present, and future wrongdoings is a gift without comparison. It is the ultimate gift.

Many people, myself included, can unequivocally say the greatest gift we've ever received is our salvation. This matchless gift assures us that all of our sins are completely forgiven and that when our earthly lives have ended, we have the full assurance of an unbroken union with God in heaven. Also, while we are still on the earth, God endows each of us with the grace to live a victorious life and triumph over all evil. Nothing we have, own, or can ever become can rival God's amazing grace. Nothing comes close to God's free pardon for our sins; all we can do is offer Him our love in return. The words from a famous hymn seem to be the most appropriate at this point: "His love has no limits, His grace has no measure, His power no boundary known unto men, for out of His infinite riches in Jesus He giveth, and giveth, and giveth again" ("*He Giveth More Grace,*" Annie J. Flint).

To avoid future disaster, we must continue to live with full trust in God's word. And, as already stated, we were created to be directly related to the Creator of the entire universe. What an awesome inheritance we have been blessed with. Our spiritual DNA is transformed when we are reborn through Jesus Christ. We once again become a part of God's eternal family. All these blessings are far too great for us to comprehend, and the immeasurable blessings given to us through Jesus Christ make us heirs of God's eternal kingdom as future citizens of heaven.

But to all who believed him and accepted him, he gave the right to become children of God. They are reborn—not with a physical birth resulting from human passion or plan, but a birth that comes from God (John 1:12–13, NLT).

Jesus replied, "I tell you the truth, unless you are born again, you cannot see the Kingdom of God" (John 3:3, NLT).

For you are all children of God through faith in Christ Jesus (Gal. 3:26, NLT).

Praise be to the God and Father of our Lord Jesus Christ, who has blessed us in the heavenly realms with every spiritual blessing in Christ (Eph. 1:3, NIV).

God's love transforms our lives. When we choose to love Him back, our hearts become good soil in which His word can grow. This causes our lives to flourish, and God's grace operating within and around us attracts human beings to God. As we lead people back to God, we will also be blessed by Him. Creation, followed by the free gift of redemption, makes God more than deserving of ultimate love. We ought to spend our precious new lives wisely, showing gratitude toward God.

By design, we were created to live being loved by God, while extending His love to one another.

After human beings accept the free gift of redemption, we become partakers in God's plan for restoring our planet. This ought to be our great joy—seeing our fellow human beings who were never designed to die being fully restored to His family and eternal life.

> All this is from God, who reconciled us to Himself through Christ and gave us the ministry of reconciliation: that God was reconciling the world to Himself in Christ, not counting men's trespasses against them. And He has committed to us the message of reconciliation. Therefore we are ambassadors for Christ, as though God were making His appeal through us. We implore you on behalf of Christ: Be reconciled to God (2 Cor. 5:18–20, NIV).

> For we are both God's workers. And you are God's field. You are God's building (1 Cor. 3:9, NLT).

We must lay hold of our new identities as sons and daughters of God and fulfill our destinies as true lovers of God. The free gift of salvation is the greatest and most awesome gift anyone can ever experience or receive. The depth of God's love is far too wonderful for us to ever grasp fully, and fidelity to His every command is great wisdom. By obeying His commands, we will avoid the deep trap of sin that ensnared Adam and Eve.

Are you willing to be in God's family as a coworker?

5

Jesus, Our Perfect Model for Giving God Ultimate Love

Giving God ultimate love is a lifetime journey. Jesus left a perfect model for us of giving God ultimate love. His life serves as the quintessential guide for our lives because He fully embodied all that is humanly achievable to honor God. When Jesus' earthly life was drawing to a close, a colossal spiritual, emotional, and physical battle lay ahead of Him. He was about to wrestle with all the forces of evil to rescue humanity from their sins, and the miserable days ahead would begin with a series of heartbreaking events.

Betrayal and abandonment by His closest friends would be the first brutal blow, followed by a severe beating at the hands of the religious leaders of the day. The final crushing blow would be suffering a gruesome death on a cross. Jesus knew all these things were about to happen but did not let the terrible impending ordeals prevent Him from worshipping God. This is our first astonishing event! Who thinks of celebrating God when they're about to face the worst moment of their lives, especially when their suffering is directly caused by obeying Him? Fear, despair, and trepidation would have gripped most of us, but in the midst of these sufferings that were prophesied before His birth, Jesus left all of humanity a matchless final lesson on loving God.

As His great sufferings were about to begin, Jesus gathered the same close companions who would soon betray or abandon Him together to enjoy their last meal as a group. When the meal ended, He led His friends in a song of worship to celebrate God, not letting His imminent death prevent Him from honoring God: "Then they sang a hymn and went out to the Mount of Olives" (Matt. 26:30, NLT).

He had started experiencing the torments that would buffet His soul, and powerful leaders abused their governmental authority to falsely accuse and prosecute Him. They brought in witnesses to make false accusations against Him, and through eyewitness accounts we have the great privilege of witnessing our Savior's struggles. As Jesus grappled with God's will for His life, our second lesson comes during the lengthy time He spent in prayer at the olive groves in the garden of Gethsemane. There Jesus would wrestle with excruciating emotional pain and face unquantifiable anguish.

On the way, Jesus told them, "Tonight all of you will desert me. For the Scriptures say, 'God will strike the Shepherd, and the sheep of the flock will be scattered.'" . . . Then Jesus went with them to the olive grove called Gethsemane, and he said, "Sit here while I go over there to pray." . . . And he became anguished and distressed. He told them, "My soul is crushed with grief to the point of death. Stay here and keep watch with me" (Matt. 26:31, 36–38, NLT).

He expressed His deep distress to His heavenly Father during the intense heart-to-heart conversations He had with Him. Our Savior was so anguished that His sweat appeared like great drops of blood, and the question of whether He would yield Himself wholly to God would be eternally and irreversibly resolved.

Then an angel from heaven appeared and strengthened him. He prayed more fervently, and he was in such agony of spirit that his sweat fell to the ground like great drops of blood (Luke 22:43–44, NLT).

Then he said to them, "My soul is overwhelmed with sorrow to the point of death" (Matt. 26:38, NIV).

He went on a little farther and bowed with his face to the ground, praying, "My Father! If it is possible, let this cup of suffering be taken away from me. Yet I want your will to be done, not mine" (Matt. 26:39, NLT).

As the unimaginable encounter with Satan and all the forces of evil ensued, Jesus did not waver in His commitment to God's purpose for His life. He was resolute throughout the gruesome ordeal, and we are allowed to observe the second greatest temptation to face humankind in this second garden, Gethsemane. The first garden was the one in Eden, where Adam and Eve caved in to the temptation to forsake God and destroyed all of creation.

During a night devoted to gut-wrenching conversations with God, Jesus finally chose to submit Himself completely to God. During this encounter, He fully demonstrated that giving God ultimate love would require far more from us than singing, dancing, celebrating, or giving gifts, as we read about earlier.

Giving God over-the-top, mega love is primarily about submitting to Him.

Jesus chose to endure a suffering so great that only God in human form could withstand it, and the stress of His sufferings were overwhelming even for Him. In the most excruciating surrender conceivable, He gave Himself over to God's perfect will for His life. Jesus chose not to flee from the known will of God, even though obeying it would bring Him extreme pain. He left us with the most outstanding illustration of giving all to God. Although it would cost Him His earthly life, He chose to obey God, so that we could receive the ultimate blessing.

God's complete and free pardon and the sacrifice that brought peace to all human beings were achieved only through Jesus' full surrender of His own will. He spent three days and nights in the darkest recesses of hell, paying for every perversion human beings will ever commit, giving up His life to restore us back into God's family. The fullest description of the punishment that Jesus accepted for us to receive forgiveness is carefully detailed in Isaiah Chapter 53.

He was despised and rejected—a man of sorrows, acquainted with deepest grief. We turned our backs on him and looked the other way. He was despised, and we did not care. Yet it was our weaknesses he carried; it was our sorrows that weighed him down. And we thought his troubles were a punishment from God, a punishment for his own sins! But he was pierced for our rebellion, crushed for our sins. He was beaten so we could be whole. He was whipped so we could be healed. All of us, like sheep, have strayed away. We have left God's paths to follow our own. Yet the Lord laid on him the sins of us all. He was oppressed and treated harshly yet he never said a word. He was led like a lamb to the slaughter. And as a sheep is silent before the shearers, he did not open his mouth. Unjustly condemned, he was led away. No one cared that he died without descendants, that his life was cut short in midstream. But he was struck down for the rebellion of my people. He had done no wrong and had never deceived anyone. But he was buried like a criminal; he was put in a rich man's grave. But it was the Lord's good plan to crush him and cause him grief. Yet when his life is made an offering for sin, he will have many descendants. He will enjoy a long life, and the Lord's good plan will prosper in his hands. When he sees all that is accomplished by his anguish, he will be satisfied. And because of his experience, my righteous servant will make it possible for many to be counted righteous, for he will bear all their sins. I will give him the honors of a victorious soldier, because he exposed himself to death. He was counted among the rebels. He bore the sins of many and interceded for rebels (Isa. 53; 3–12, NLT).

For our sakes, the Savior of the world bravely took upon Himself the full penalty for all of humankind's sins. He secured eternal salvation for everyone who would accept Him and, in the rarest display of mega, over-the-top love for God, Jesus walked in full obedience to God regardless of the cost. If we are ever in a situation that requires a full surrender from us like His, will we still be able to trust and have full faith in God? Choosing to give God our obedience in such moments brings God the most precious spiritual sacrifice.

When we surrender our lives to God by loving and esteeming Him in the midst of stifling and mystifying life occurrences, we give Him the rarest love offering possible. When our all is requested of us or appears to be brutally snatched away, as was the case with a man named Job, will we give God our total trust at all times? This is the final frontier of giving God ultimate love.

A truly submitted life is the highest way we can give God our unsurpassable love.

Jesus paid the ultimate price when He offered His life as the perfect sacrifice for our sins. The lessons He left behind give us a behind-the-scenes look into God's love for humankind. Those who came before us revealed God's accessibility. He is available to anyone who chooses to seek Him, whether they be king or pauper, great or small. We'll learn throughout our study that God grants great deliverance and awesome favors to those who place their unwavering trust in Him.

He is not far from each one of us. For in Him
we live and move and have our being. As some

of your own poets have said, "We are His offspring" (Acts 17:27–28, BSB).

*God is not far from any one of us. His ears are always
open to His children. He is the ever-near God. How will you
respond to His love?*

6

A Passionate Praise Dance for God Ends a Royal Marriage!

K ing David had replaced royal robes with humble priestly garments as he twirled, leaped, celebrated, and rejoiced before God with total abandon. His unparalleled display of love for God is one of my favorite examples of humility and courage. David unashamedly danced in the streets to honor God when Israel returned the ark of the covenant to its place in Jerusalem. He did not let the dignity and protocols that normally accompany being the sovereign deter him from humbling himself before God; instead, he chose to personally lead the people in worship as they brought the ark that symbolized God's presence to its rightful place.

David personally oversaw and participated in every detail of the process, and his actions elevated the importance of the occasion in the people's hearts. His devotion to God helped everyone focus on the sacredness of their gathering, and they all worshipped in unity. David was so determined to make the occasion wholly about God that he offered sacrifices with every few steps that were taken. As they went along during the great procession, he did not care how he looked to others but danced passionately for an audience of one: God.

> And so it was, that when the bearers of the ark of the LORD had gone six paces, he sacrificed an ox and a fatling. And David was dancing before the LORD with all his might, and David was wearing a linen ephod. So David and all the house of Israel were bringing up the ark of the LORD with shouting and the sound of the trumpet (2 Sam. 6:14–15, NASB).

David disregarded the opinions of others while giving God his best to the point of getting into trouble with his wife! Princess Michal happened to be looking out of the window as the great procession went by and caught a glimpse of her husband dancing vigorously for the Lord on the streets below. She felt so embarrassed that she instantly despised him in her heart. Her attitude toward David was total disdain, and as soon as he got home she expressed her strong disapproval.

Michal unleashed a hot rebuke against David, making her extreme displeasure at his extravagant display of love for God abundantly clear. But by insulting her husband's worship, she had also insulted and dishonored God. Her actions permanently damaged their marriage, and this incident made Michal barren for the rest of her life.

> Then it happened as the ark of the LORD came into the city of David that Michal the daughter of Saul looked out of the window and saw King David leaping and dancing before the LORD; and she despised him in her heart ... But when David returned to bless his household, Michal the daughter of Saul came out to meet David and said, "How the king of Israel distinguished himself today! He uncovered himself today in the eyes of his servants' maids as one of the foolish ones shamelessly uncovers himself!" So David said to Michal, "It was before the LORD, who chose me above your father and above all his house, to appoint me ruler over the people of the LORD, over Israel; therefore I will celebrate before the LORD." I will be more lightly esteemed than this and will be humble in my own eyes, but with the maids of whom you have spoken, with them I will be distinguished." Michal the daughter of Saul had no child to the day of her death (2 Sam. 6:16, 6:20–23, NASB).

Although no child was ever born to the two of them, David went on to receive many rewards from God for his great devotion. And one must wonder why Michal wasn't in this sacred procession during a national event to honor God alongside her husband. Surely on such a special day, a princess of the realm ought to have been present. While David was busy rejoicing in and loving God, his wife was totally ignoring and disregarding Him.

This auspicious occasion proved that Michal was not a true lover or worshipper of God. She was at the wrong location at the wrong time with the wrong mind-set. By not honoring the leader God had chosen, she had also despised God. There are many reasons to lavish our over-the-top love on God, and when we finally lose our fear of people, we will be able to give to God something extremely precious to Him: our ultimate love.

Giving God our ultimate love may bring us some suffering, but God is very pleased when we honor Him. Giving God extravagant love will also cost us something. It may be our wealth, self-importance, cherished relationships, or some other thing. But God promises us many rewards for our faithfulness to Him. Just like any loving parent, God delights in blessing us back. David's love for God made him a great leader; he understood that honoring God produces unquantifiable blessings in our lives. During his reign, he appointed special leaders to take care of God's business first.

David appointed the following Levites to lead the people in worship before the Ark of the LORD—to invoke his blessings, to give thanks, and to praise the LORD, the God of Israel (1 Chron. 16:4, NLT).

The many blessings in David's life resulted directly from his sincere love for God. Genuine affection for God flowed from his heart, and this brought the nation many benefits. God gave them rest from all their enemies and protected them from all harm. He also blessed David with many spectacular promises regarding his posterity, and all of these blessings were because of their leader's great love for God. Israel is still renowned throughout the earth today, and the world continues to be positively impacted by this tiny messianic nation.

Now it came about when the king lived in his house, and the LORD had given him rest on every side from all his enemies . . . [The LORD said,] "I have been with you wherever you have gone and have cut off all your enemies from before you; and I will make you a great name, like the names of the great men who are on the earth. I will also appoint a place for My people Israel and will plant them, that they may live in their own place and not be disturbed again, nor will the wicked afflict them any more as formerly, even from the day that I commanded judges to be over My people Israel; and I will give you rest from all your enemies. The LORD also declares to you that the LORD will make a house for you. When your days are complete and you lie down with your fathers, I will raise up your descendant after you, who will come forth from you, and I will establish his kingdom. He shall build a house for My name, and I will establish the throne of his kingdom forever. . . . Your house and your kingdom shall endure before Me forever; your throne shall be established forever" (2 Sam. 7:1, 9–13, 16, NASB).

David did not offer his extravagant worship to God in order to receive anything from Him. He simply wanted to express his love to Him the best way he knew how. God, however, cannot be outdone. Whatsoever a man sows, he will reap. The Lord responded to David's lavish display of love for Him with awesome fruits and great promises. God's reaction to his devotion took David himself by surprise. He had not expected any form of reward for his love for God, and when confronted with God's goodness, David reacted the only way he knew how: with some more worship, of course! Outpourings of love toward God flowed from David's heart toward God as he thanked Him profusely for His magnanimity toward him and his imperfect family. We observe the sincerity of David's heart after he had reaped unexpected fruits from his great love for God in the following verses:

> Then David the king went in and sat before the LORD, and he said, "Who am I, O Lord GOD, and what is my house, that You have brought me this far? And yet this was insignificant in Your eyes, O Lord GOD, for You have spoken also of the house of Your servant concerning the distant future. And this is the custom of man, O Lord GOD. Again what more can David say to You? For You know Your servant, O Lord GOD! For the sake of Your word, and according to Your own heart, You have done all this greatness to let Your servant know. For this reason You are great, O Lord God; for there is none like You, and there is no God besides You, according to all that we have heard with our ears (2 Sam 7:18–22, NASB).

In 2 Samuel 5:17–20, we also learn another great lesson from King David at the beginning of his reign. Israel's enemies, the Philistines, found out that David had been appointed as the nation's new king and gathered a great army to fight against him. They sought to stop the advance of the nation before the new leader could establish himself, trying to prevent Israel from gaining supremacy in the region. The kingdom of darkness, in the form of the Philistine army, came against God's forces of light, in the form of Israel's army. But such was the relationship between God and David that the immediate response from this lover of God was to go privately into God's presence to seek His help. He did not look to the nation's military leaders or its skilled tacticians for their battle strategy but went directly to the true source of strength and power: God Himself.

The Philistines failed to recognize God's presence (a fruit of worship) in David's life, and this led to their downfall. The destruction of their army was so complete that they could not have seen it coming. God will never, ever disappoint us when we place our trust in Him. He gave David a resounding victory over his enemies every time he sought Him, and during David's entire reign the king's name became a terror to all his enemies. The surrounding nations greatly feared Israel's new king, and it is noteworthy that Israel's greatest warrior also showed the greatest love for God.

David was also a great psalmist. He loved God and wrote many songs about Him that documented their great relationship.

> Bless the LORD, O my soul,
> and all that is within me,
> bless his holy name!
> Bless the LORD, O my soul,
> and forget not all his benefits,

who forgives all your iniquity,
who heals all your diseases,
who redeems your life from the pit,
who crowns you with steadfast love and mercy,
who satisfies you with good
so that your youth is renewed like the eagle's
(Ps. 103:1-5, ESV).

David's love for the Lord produced much fruitfulness in his life, including the qualities of boldness, courage, and might. This led to so many victories for Israel. This king's deep intimacy with God also gave him outstanding prophetic insight. He constantly sought the Lord when developing fresh strategies for each battle and never relied solely on his own ability or past victories. King David continued to receive fresh revelation and wisdom from God for each new conflict. This was the source of his confidence and power. The 44th psalm from the Book of Psalms, composed by the sons of Korah, speaks of confident prayer for God's victory when Israel called out to Him for rescue.

You are my King, O God;
Command victories for Jacob.
Through You we will push back our adversaries;
Through Your name we will trample down those who rise up against us.
For I will not trust in my bow,

Nor will my sword save me.
But You have saved us from our adversaries,
And You have put to shame those who hate us.
In God we have boasted all day long,
And we will give thanks to Your name forever
(Ps. 44:4-8, NASB).

David frequently displayed patient dependency on God, and his life gives us further examples of the blessings found in a life that loves, honors, and serves God. The king would not move before God moved, and unlike his predecessor, King Saul, David was completely dependent upon God for help. Receiving help from God must also be our own expectation during our struggles. The fruit of holy boldness produced in a life that trusts God will propel us into victory when we love God.

So let us come boldly to the throne of our gracious God. There we will receive his mercy, and we will find grace to help us when we need it most (Heb. 4:16, NLT).

The intimacy that develops between us and the Lord will remove all our doubts and banish our fears. We must also remember that our relationship with God is not one-sided. When we put Him in first place and spend time with Him, His blessings become manifest in our lives and overflow into the lives around us.

King David's heart for God cost him his marriage to Michal and brought harsh criticism against him. Whose opinion should we care the most about when giving God extravagant love?

7

This Leader Takes Things to a Whole New Level

As we just read, King David received abundant blessings from the Lord as fruits of his devotion. His son Solomon would take things to a whole new level after his death. As a part of his extravagant worship, King David, before he died, had meticulously prepared abundant gifts for the building of a spectacular temple for the Lord. His son Solomon used those gifts to build the most impressive house of worship ever recorded in human history. According to modern research, the gold and silver used for the building, if converted to today's money, would equal *$216,603,576,000!* This does not include the other precious metals, bronze, iron, ivory, cedar, or other materials used for the construction of this elaborate edifice.

Then David said, "This will be the location for the Temple of the Lord God and the place of the altar for Israel's burnt offerings!" So David gave orders to call together the foreigners living in Israel, and he assigned them the task of preparing finished stone for building the Temple of God. David provided large amounts of iron for the nails that would be needed for the doors in the gates and for the clamps, and he gave more bronze than could be weighed. He also provided innumerable cedar logs, for the men of Tyre and Sidon had brought vast amounts of cedar to David. David said, "My son Solomon is still young and inexperienced. And since the Temple to be built for the Lord must be a magnificent structure, famous and glorious throughout the world, I will begin making preparations for it now." So David collected vast amounts of building materials before his death (1 Chron. 22:1–5, NLT).

God created everything and gives life to everyone. He alone truly deserves our very best. Believing that God deserves only the leftovers of our lives is erroneous thinking. Worldly people make no apologies for spending huge fortunes on athletes, music, big-budget movies, or other items they deem necessary for their enjoyment and delight. They frequently purchase dazzling jewelry, million-dollar mansions, expensive cars, designer clothing, rare paintings and treasures, and just about anything that catches their fancy.

Using their wealth to express love for God is rarely done, yet He is the only one worthy of our ultimate love in every way. From the beginning of his reign, Solomon followed in his father's footsteps and left us another awe-inspiring illustration of extravagant worship. King Solomon donated innumerable offerings during the dedication of this magnificent temple built just for the Lord, and his offerings were the largest ever recorded in human history!

David's son went all out in joyful worship of God after finishing and furnishing the building, and the new king's magnanimous sacrifices were accompanied with jubilant praises and music. This celebration of God went on for days. Wow! When was the last time anyone stayed at church for several days just to love and worship God? David's love for God had been exemplary, and Solomon did not let the family down.

Our children and other loved ones will also learn to honor God by our example.

Then the king and all the people offered sacrifice before the LORD. King Solomon offered a sacrifice of 22,000 oxen and 120,000 sheep. Thus the king and all the people dedicated the house of God. The priests stood at their posts,

and the Levites also, with the instruments of
music to the LORD, which King David had
made for giving praise to the LORD—"for His
lovingkindness is everlasting"—whenever he
gave praise by their means, while the priests
on the other side blew trumpets; and all Israel
was standing. Then Solomon consecrated the
middle of the court that was before the house of
the LORD, for there he offered the burnt offerings and the fat of the peace offerings because
the bronze altar which Solomon had made was
not able to contain the burnt offering, the grain
offering and the fat. So Solomon observed the
feast at that time for seven days, and all Israel
with him, a very great assembly who came from
the entrance of Hamath to the brook of Egypt.
On the eighth day they held a solemn assembly, for the dedication of the altar they observed
seven days and the feast seven days (2 Chron.
7:4–9, NASB).

David's son Solomon also prioritized waiting on the
Lord right after he ascended his father's throne, and he
made the choice to seek God for His immediate and con-
tinuous help. Although authority had been legitimately
transferred to him on the earth, King Solomon demonstrated that he knew that God was the true source of
wisdom and power. By asking the Lord for the wisdom

to lead His people right, Solomon was following in his faithful father's footsteps. Always seek God first and not last in all of your endeavors.

Solomon did not place confidence in his pedigree as a king's son or try to claim the previous achievements of his great warrior father. Instead, he humbled himself before God and asked Him for His guidance. Well, Solomon also received far more from God than he could ever have asked for!

> Now to him who is able to do immeasurably more than all we ask or imagine, according to his power that is at work within us (Eph. 3:20, NIV).

> Solomon went up there before the LORD to the bronze altar which was at the tent of meeting, and offered a thousand burnt offerings on it. In that night God appeared to Solomon and said to him, "Ask what I shall give you." Solomon said to God, "You have dealt with my father David with great loving kindness, and have made me king in his place. Now, O LORD God, Your promise to my father David is fulfilled, for You have made me king over a people as numerous as the dust of the earth. Give me now wisdom and knowledge, that I may go out and come in before this people, for who can rule this

great people of Yours?" God said to Solomon, "Because you had this in mind, and did not ask for riches, wealth or honor, or the life of those who hate you, nor have you even asked for long life, but you have asked for yourself wisdom and knowledge that you may rule My people over whom I have made you king, wisdom and knowledge have been granted to you. And I will give you riches and wealth and honor, such as none of the kings who were before you has possessed nor those who will come after you" (2 Chron. 1:6–12, NASB).

Then the Lord appeared to Solomon at night and said to him, "I have heard your prayer and have chosen this place for Myself as a house of sacrifice. If I shut up the heavens so that there is no rain, or if I command the locust to devour the land, or if I send pestilence among My people, and My people who are called by My name humble themselves and pray and seek My face and turn from their wicked ways, then I will hear from heaven, will forgive their sin and will heal their land" (2 Chron. 7:12–14, NASB).

God granted Solomon both what he had asked for—wisdom and knowledge—and what he had not requested—riches, wealth, and honor. "Moreover, I will give you what you have not asked for—both wealth and honor—so that in your lifetime you will have no equal among kings" (1 Kings 3:13, NIV). These were all fruits of Solomon's love for and worship of God. God will richly bless anyone who diligently and sincerely seeks to love and honor Him. He gives them far more than they could ever ask or think.

All these things happened after Solomon prioritized honoring God first and offered Him over-the-top, mega love during his extravagant worship at the dedication of the new temple. No king before or after Solomon would ever possess the wealth and precious gifts that God bestowed on Solomon. Just like his father before him, Solomon received far more fruit for his devotion than he could ever have imagined or asked for. The new king also received many new promises from God apart from the ones given to his father, David. This again reminds us that the grace to successfully accomplish all that we aspire to do is found in God. The humility and love these two leaders displayed toward God revealed that they were true lovers of God. We also need to rely on God and not solely on our own abilities. Access to true success is obtained, maintained, and retained by loving and abiding in God.

How will we express our own mega love for God? Are you ready to receive mega blessings from Him?

8

Worshipping God Is Showing Him Mega Love

Part of our definition of love earlier was "tenderness, fondness, adoration, worship, or devotion." We can easily relate to tenderness, fondness, and adoration with regard to loving someone. But what does worship have to do with love and giving God mega love? Reading about King David's love for God and how this affected his worship raises this question: Is there any relationship or connection between love and worship? To answer this, let's examine the meaning of *worship*. It comes from two old English words: *weorth*, which means worth, and *ship*. Worth-ship is the quality of having worth or being of value, "worthiness."

Webster's 1828 dictionary defines worship as "honor with extravagant love and extreme submission; as a lover." Worship is also defined as "adore, pay divine

honors to, reverence with supreme respect and venera-
tion," and "perform acts of adoration."

Honor means "regard with great respect, highly
esteem; admire and devote oneself to."

So within the definition of worship are these two
words that relate to giving God over-the-top, mega love:
extravagant love. This informs us that love is directly connected to worship, and that the two words, under many
circumstances, are interchangeable. Worshipping God is
loving Him, and extravagantly loving Him is the true
essence of worship. When we express our desire to give
God ultimate love, it is the same as giving Him ultimate
worship.

To worship someone or something is to give your
heart to serve that person or thing. To love God genuinely, as we seek to do, we must learn to hold Him in
the highest esteem and extravagantly love Him, which
is worship.

The overflowing of love and thanksgiving in our
hearts for His great love toward us will move us to
want to express our love to Him as worship. Someone
remarked, as I shared about this topic, that worshipping God is like giving Him over-the-top, mega love!
Everyone desires to be loved, and God is no exception.
Our desire to give God our best is rooted in our love for
Him. Worship is the most intimate expression of love
and devotion toward God. Moses, the great lawgiver and
leader of Israel, sang these words of adoration to God

for His great mercies toward Israel. His song is again repeated in the New Testament.

For I proclaim the name of the LORD;
Ascribe greatness to our God!
The Rock! His work is perfect,
For all His ways are just;
A God of faithfulness and without injustice,
Righteous and upright is He (Deut. 32:3-4, NASB).

[And they] sang the song of God's servant Moses and of the Lamb:
"Great and marvelous are your deeds,
    Lord God Almighty.
Just and true are your ways,
    King of the nations" (Rev. 15:3, BSB).

As we learned earlier, King David delighted in the Lord and prioritized worship above any other activity in his nation. His words have been set to music that is widely used during worship services worldwide, and according to David, worship should be expressed not only by those who have been saved and redeemed by God but also by every creature God has made.

Let everything that breathes sing praises to the Lord! Praise the Lord! (Ps. 150:6, NLT).

"Shout for joy to the Lord, all the earth, burst into jubilant song with music (Ps. 98:4, NIV).

Let the whole earth sing to the Lord! Each day proclaim the good news that he saves (1 Chron. 16:23, NLT).

His words reveal that we should not confine expressing love to God to the four walls of any church. Everything that breathes must take part in this awesome mega-lovefest too! God's family on earth joins His family in heaven to offer our awesome Creator never-ending symphonies of praise as we beautify and magnify the ever-living self-existing Creator with the fruit of our lips: giving thanks. We come together to worship the One who created us, thanking Him for who He is and all He has done. Giving glory to the One who loved us first, we testify to all His wonderful works and shower Him with our love.

Through Jesus, therefore, let us continually offer to God a sacrifice of praise—the fruit of lips that openly profess his name (Heb. 13:15, NIV).

Make thankfulness your sacrifice to God, and keep the vows you made to the Most High (Ps. 50:14, NIV).

By proclaiming God's miraculous deeds and declaring all His marvelous acts for everyone to know, we are demonstrating our love for Him and telling everyone how altogether awesome He is. Love songs are usually written and sung to express our love to that very special someone. Singing, dancing, speaking out, and applauding God are also ways that we can express our deep affection to Him. Using all kinds of instruments to honor God, we bring our freewill offerings of worship to Him.

Sing to the Lord a new song; sing to the Lord, all the earth (Ps. 96:1, NIV).

I will praise the Lord, and may everyone on earth bless his holy name forever and ever (Ps. 145:21, NLT).

All the nations you made will come and bow before you, Lord; they will praise your holy name. For you are great and perform wonderful deeds. You alone are God (Ps. 86:9–10, NLT).

With hearts free from pretense, let's glorify God and let His praises ring throughout the earth! Declare His great worth to as many people as you can and wholeheartedly convey your love to the one who gave us life because of His great love. The more we appreciate who God is, the greater our love for Him will be. According

to the scriptures, the earth was without form, light, or
life before the beginning of creation. God brought everything into existence by His word, out of immense love.
He filled our dark, dreary planet with light, vegetation,
and life, and a once-empty space was dramatically transformed by God's magnificent creation.

> In the beginning God created the heavens and
> the earth. The earth was formless and void, and
> darkness was over the surface of the deep, and
> the Spirit of God was moving over the surface
> of the waters. Then God said, "Let there be
> light"; and there was light (Gen. 1:1–3, NASB).

> For "the earth is the LORD's, and everything in
> it." . . . For God, who said, "Let there be light in
> the darkness," has made this light shine in our
> hearts so we could know the glory of God that
> is seen in the face of Jesus Christ (1 Cor. 10:26,
> 2 Cor. 4:6, NLT).

Showing our gratitude and affection to God, who
is our loving heavenly Father, is the rightful and joyful
duty of His loving children. Celebrating God daily by
presenting our lives to Him as a living sacrifice honors
Him. This is our true and proper worship, a unique way
for human beings to give Him our over-the-top, mega
love. "Therefore, I urge you, brothers and sisters, in view

of God's mercy, to offer your bodies as a living sacrifice, holy and pleasing to God—this is your true and proper worship" (Rom. 12:1, NIV).

In light of the interchangeable nature between love and worship, how then can we give God ultimate worship that would meet our criteria for giving Him ultimate love? Let's contemplate a few ideas together. Could a spectacular event designed solely for and about Him, consisting of only the best and most unique voices on the earth, fit the bill? Or maybe a colossal, record-breaking, mega-sized choir in the largest gathering ever put together to honor the Lord?

How many people would this require, and what instruments and technologies would be involved? This idea immediately poses a problem, because if giving God ultimate love requires super-large numbers or rare and unique talents, then most people would not be able to attempt this. Also where, when, and how would such a great event take place, and who among us is qualified to lead such a colossal gathering? Let's think of a few more ideas.

How about an excessively large donation given exclusively to the Lord's work or to the poor? Would this qualify as an ultimate expression of love for Him? Or perhaps a special act of service performed purely for His sake. How about an exceptional piece of artwork commissioned and dedicated exclusively to the Lord? Or maybe a carefully crafted song written for and about

Him? But many songs have already been written in so many ways and languages. This might not seem special enough to meet our criterion of ultimate.

Could we perhaps qualify by setting ourselves apart to be alone with God in special lengthy times of consecration with prayer and fasting or by devoting ourselves to full-time ministry? Could this meet the highest standard of loving, honoring, and serving Him? This idea also immediately poses a problem, because not every believer is called into full-time service or ministry, but every single one of us is destined for worship.

> Come, everyone! Clap your hands! Shout to God with joyful praise! (Ps. 47:1, NLT).

> Since we are receiving a Kingdom that is unshakeable, let us be thankful and please God by worshipping him with holy fear and awe (Heb. 12:28, NLT).

How then do we give ultimate worship to God so we can give Him mega love? Many of these ideas seem too small by comparison to the greatness of our recipient, God. Is it even possible to give God ultimate worship and, if so, how exactly do we go about doing this? More suggestions may come to your own mind as we all attempt to come up with different ways to fulfill our stated mission of giving God ultimate love.

I admitted earlier that giving God our over-the-top, mega love or worship might sound like a formidable goal. To add to the magnitude of the task I have set before us, I'd like to draw our attention to an amazing event recorded in the book of Revelation. We are given a rare glimpse into an awesome worship gathering of such tremendous size that the numbers involved are simply staggering! It is what can only be described as a majestic symphony of love for the Creator and is quite a captivating image.

> Then I looked and heard the voice of many angels, numbering thousands upon thousands, and ten thousand times ten thousand. They encircled the throne and the living creatures and the elders. In a loud voice they were saying: "Worthy is the Lamb, who was slain, to receive power and wealth and wisdom and strength and honor and glory and praise!" Then I heard every creature in heaven and on earth and under the earth and on the sea, and all that is in them, saying: "To him who sits on the throne and to the Lamb be praise and honor and glory and power, for ever and ever!" The four living creatures said, "Amen," and the elders fell down and worshiped (Rev. 5:11–14, NIV).

What could we give to God that can possibly com-
pare to what we've just read? This is the greatest lovefest
ever held in honor of God the Creator. The participants
join in from multiple locations in both the heavens and
the earth, and from what we've just read, we learn that
God has at least one hundred million angels! These
majestic beings adore and worship God round the clock,
and although we don't have any specifics on how many
angels God has created, He may have untold thousands
besides these. Their numbers may be comparable only to
the number of stars in the universe, and that could run
into the billions! These heavenly beings, along with all
the other creatures God has made—more than we can
ever imagine—join together to take part in this greatest
worship gathering ever to honor God.

The huge numbers involved and the awesome talents of the participants make this an impossible act to
follow! All these glorious voices unquestionably surpass
anything human beings can put together on the earth,
and this one event puts our idea of a colossal, mega-sized
choir to honor God in the shade. After we read about
this amazing event, it would not be wrong to question
whether we can ever give God ultimate worship here on
the earth. This awe-inspiring gathering surpasses anything we could ever come up with, and we may think it's
time to give up on this part of our mission. You may feel
a bit deflated, thinking we can never give God ultimate
love, but I have some good news!

An in-depth look through the scriptures lets us know that giving God ultimate love is not unrealizable. In fact, the Bible affirms our ability to accomplish this mission. While we recover from any discouraging thoughts regarding our goal, what joy these following words bring:

> For where two or three gather together as my followers, I am there among them (Matt. 18:20, NLT).

> And surely I am with you always, to the very end of the age (Matt. 28:20, NIV).

These words recalibrate our minds by telling us that loving, honoring, and worshipping God has nothing at all to do with large numbers or massive crowds. God does not require extraordinary feats or huge sacrifices to please Him. Enjoying our union with God has nothing to do with the size of our churches and congregations, so to understand what God considers ultimate love or worship, we must look further into His word.

If millions, thousands, or even hundreds of people are not needed to express ultimate love or worship to God, what on earth will merit that term? I must again quickly caution that, although our desire to give God mega love is noble, we should not in any way treat the intimate expression of love or worship as a contest to be

God's favorites or trivialize it in any way. We are also
encouraged in the Bible to come together regularly to
express our love to God and honor Him with psalms,
hymns, and spiritual songs from our hearts. We are
encouraged to continually provoke one another to "acts
of love and good works," of which giving God our over-
the-top love would be number one.

> Let us think of ways to motivate one another
> to acts of love and good works. And let us not
> neglect our meeting together, as some people
> do, but encourage one another, especially now
> that the day of his return is drawing near (Heb.
> 10:24–25, NLT).

> Be filled with the Spirit, speaking to one another
> with psalms, hymns, and songs from the Spirit.
> Sing and make music from your heart to the
> Lord, always giving thanks to God the Father
> for everything, in the name of our Lord Jesus
> Christ (Eph. 5:18–20, NIV).

*Since extravagantly loving God is the same as
extravagantly worshipping Him, how can we give God
extravagant worship?*

CHAPTER

9

Giving God Our
Obedience Is Loving Him

L et's take a closer look at the second part of the
definition of worship we just looked at to answer
the last question posed: How do we honor God with
extreme submission? When God's Holy Spirit fills our
hearts with His love, He helps us to submit to God. The
scriptures teach us that our obedience to God demon-
strates love and respect for Him because He has clearly
demonstrated His love for us. Given the choice to love
and freely follow Him, a redeemed person ought to
respond with obedience to His word. This is one of the
major ways that we also can give God our mega love.

Obedience is the exact opposite of defiant resistance
to God, or rebelliousness. God's word is good for us and
good with us.

God's unconditional love drove Him to surrender
His all to rescue us. We did nothing to deserve Jesus'
taking the full responsibility for all of our sins. God's

actions prove the depths of His amazing grace, and our world desperately needs God. If we will choose to grow into God's likeness by obeying Him, we develop His nature, which is love. This enables us to become helpers of His joy on the earth.

The yoke of sin and hopelessness that previously choked our lives is completely destroyed by Jesus' sacrifice on the cross. All things have become new in our lives, and abundant life, hope, faith, and joy are fully restored to everyone who believes. Through His Son Jesus Christ, God obliterates the guilt of our sin and all of its power over us. If we continue obeying God, we will remain and abide in His love forever.

Jesus instructs us that we are to keep God's commands because that is truly loving Him. Let us continue to obey God and grow in godliness, becoming more and more like our heavenly Father in character. Extreme submission means that we daily choose to align ourselves with God's commands rather than defy them.

> Those who accept my commandments and obey them are the ones who love me. And because they love me, my Father will love them. And I will love them and reveal myself to each of them (John 14:21, NLT).

> If you keep my commands, you will remain in my love, just as I have kept my Father's commands

and remain in his love (John 15:10, NIV).

We know that God doesn't listen to sinners, but he is ready to hear those who worship him and do his will (John 9:31, NLT).

When we yield to God, we are submitting to love, and people around us will be able to experience God's love through us. God is the ultimate loving parent. His Word (scripture) is our training manual. He is worthy of our obedience. The Bible also contains love letters to God's children, and the keys to a successful life are contained within them. When we give God the rightful place in our hearts, He promises to make His home within us.

Jesus replied, "Anyone who loves me will obey my teaching. My Father will love them, and we will come to them and make our home with them" (John 14:23, NIV).

You can make this choice by loving the LORD your God, obeying him, and committing yourself firmly to him. This is the key to your life. And if you love and obey the LORD, you will live long in the land the LORD swore to give your ancestors Abraham, Isaac, and Jacob (Deut. 30:20, NIV).

By loving God and being a blessing to all who come in contact with us, we partner with God to bring His love and healing to our broken planet. But when we rebel against Him, our lives become everything we don't want them to be. Our wrong actions come from our old fallen, satanic nature and evil belief systems, but the scriptures reveal to us who God is and how humankind ought to behave toward Him and one another.

All this is from God, who reconciled us to himself through Christ and gave us the ministry of reconciliation (2 Cor. 5:18, NIV).

So we are Christ's ambassadors; God is making his appeal through us. We speak for Christ when we plead, "Come back to God!" (2 Cor. 5:20, NLT).

Samuel, Israel's prophet and judge, once had to tell the nation's first king, Saul, that God was greatly displeased with him. King Saul had disobeyed the instructions God had given to Him and subsequently lost his position of great authority. After Saul had provoked God's displeasure, Samuel spoke the following words to the king, outlining the punishment and consequences that he would receive:

What is more pleasing to the Lord: your burnt offerings and sacrifices or your obedience to his voice? Listen! Obedience is better than sacrifice, and submission is better than offering the fat of rams. For rebellion is like the sin of divination, and arrogance like the evil of idolatry. Because you have rejected the word of the Lord, he has rejected you as king (1 Sam. 15:22, NLT, 1 Sam. 15:23, NIV).

Every act of disobedience or defiance toward God has very negative repercussions in our lives.

Whether we are great or small in our own eyes or in the eyes of others, there is no room for anyone to disobey God. Trusting and obeying Him is a vital part of our relationship with God and is the essential way that we demonstrate our love for Him. When we willingly submit our ways to God, it releases the power of His Holy Spirit to work in and through our lives and transform us into God's loving nature. And the more we become like God, the more His blessings will flow in every area of our lives.

We are often reminded in the scriptures that our old sinful nature can lead us back to depravity if we allow ourselves to rebel against God. We certainly do not want to reap the awful consequences that our forebears did when they deviated from God's commands. We also must not continue to contribute to the confusion we see in our world today. Because human beings have disobeyed God, we have become slaves to sin. The scriptures tell us that we become slaves to whomever and whatever we choose to obey. When we choose to obey God, we are set free from all bondage to sin and its evil consequences.

"Don't you realize that you become the slave of whatever you choose to obey? You can be a slave to sin, which leads to death, or you can choose to obey God, which leads to righteous living" (Rom. 6:16, NLT).

Jesus replied, "Very truly I tell you, everyone who sins is a slave to sin . . . . If the Son sets you free, you will be free indeed (John 8:34, 36, NIV).

Many of God's children will fail to fulfil their God-given destinies because they rejected God's teachings in the Bible. His words are for our safety, protection, and guidance. The dire consequences Adam and Eve suffered for their disobedience ought to warn us that rejecting God's word only leads to terrible outcomes. By continuously repeating our erroneous choices, we human beings have brought colossal evil to our planet. The evil consequences we see all around us of disobeying God should be the only wakeup call we need to start obeying God's word. God also promises overflowing joy as a result of our obedience to Him.

We grow and become more like Christ when we submit to our heavenly Father's love, as Jesus did. It cannot be overstated that God loves us more than we can ever fathom, and He is worthy of our ultimate love. I pray that His grace will enable each one of us to overcome our fears and gladly place our trust in Him. Obedience to God proves we are His offspring. God's commands are not to be ignored and are entirely for our own good.

When you obey my commandments, you remain in my love, just as I obey my Father's commandments and remain in his love. I have told you these things so that you will be filled with my joy. Yes, your joy will overflow (John 15:10–11, NLT).

From God's viewpoint, obedience is true worship and believing is doing. Are you willing and ready to yield to God in all your ways, or only in some of your ways?

10

Uncommon Obedience Produces Uncommon Blessings: Abraham

Abraham, who is regarded as the great father of our faith, is one of the Bible's most dramatic examples of loving, obeying, and placing unshakeable trust in God. His willingness to surrender all to God was tested to the max. His amazing journey began when God asked him to leave his place of birth, people, and family to go to a new place that God Himself would show him.

> The Lord had said to Abram, "Go from your country, your people and your father's household to the land I will show you. I will make you into a great nation, and I will bless you; I will make your name great, and you will be a blessing" (Gen. 12:1–2, NIV).

It was by faith that Abraham obeyed when God called him to leave home and go to another land that God would give him as his inheritance. He went without knowing where he was going (Heb. 11:8, NLT).

After Abraham obeyed this initial command, God made a covenant with him and pronounced a very special blessing over his life. His wife Sarah, who was also a faithful follower of God, accompanied her husband throughout their faith journeys. Although they were faithful followers of God, Abraham and Sarah were barren. They had sought the Lord for many years for the fruit of the womb, but nothing changed in their circumstances. This, however, did not diminish their love for God. They had also become so old that any expectation of ever having their own offspring was long gone. However, man's impossibilities are not impossible with God! Abraham did not give up on God's promise but continued to believe in Him.

Without weakening in his faith, he acknowledged the decrepitness of his body (since he was about a hundred years old) and the lifelessness of Sarah's womb. Yet he did not waver through disbelief in the promise of God, but was strengthened in his faith and gave glory to God, being fully persuaded that God was able to do what He had promised (Rom. 4:19–21, BSB).

After they had waited for many agonizing years and were still unable to bear a child, the couple made an unwise but understandable decision. They attempted to fulfill God's promise through their own efforts. The two arranged for a surrogate mother, Hagar, one of Sarah's maids, to bear Abraham's children. Their plan appeared to have succeeded when Hagar produced a son for Abraham. They named the boy Ishmael, which means God listens, but all did not go well with the couple after this event.

Hagar became haughty and started to disrespect Sarah. This episode reveals that even the greatest giants of faith were frail human beings like us. We sometimes grow weary of waiting for God, but when we attempt to bring God's promises to pass through our own efforts, the outcomes will be negative. Hagar and Ishmael suffered terribly for their regrettable choices and went through a series of extremely difficult events. (See Genesis 16:3–16, 21:8–21.)

After Abraham and Sarah dealt with the negative consequences of having a child through Hagar, which included sending the woman and her son away, God displayed His wonders in their lives! Although they were both well past childbearing age, Sarah suddenly conceived and gave birth to their son, whom they named Isaac, which means laughter. It was a spectacular miracle in their lives, and the fulfilment of a word God had given to Abraham a year earlier. Humanly speaking, there was not the remotest possibility they could ever have conceived a child, but man's impossibilities have never stopped the hand of God.

> He said, "I will surely return to you at this time next year; and behold, Sarah your wife will have a son." And Sarah was listening at the tent door, which was behind him. Now Abraham and Sarah were old, advanced in age; Sarah was past childbearing. Sarah laughed to herself, saying, "After I have become old, shall I have pleasure, my lord being old also?" And the LORD said to Abraham, "Why did Sarah laugh, saying, 'Shall I indeed bear a child, when I am so old?' Is anything too difficult for the LORD? At the appointed time I will return to you, at this time next year, and Sarah will have a son" (Gen. 18:10–14, NASB).

> So Abraham said to God, "May Ishmael live under your special blessing!" But God replied, "No—Sarah, your wife, will give birth to a son for you. You will name him Isaac, and I will confirm my covenant with him and his descendants as an everlasting covenant" (Gen. 17:18–19, NASB).

Then the LORD took note of Sarah as He had said, and the LORD did for Sarah as He had promised. So Sarah conceived and bore a son to Abraham in his old age, at the appointed time of which God had spoken to him. Abraham called the name of his son who was born to him, whom Sarah bore to him, Isaac (Gen. 21:1–3, NASB).

For example, there was God's promise to Abraham. Since there was no one greater to swear by, God took an oath in his own name, saying: "I will certainly bless you, and I will multiply your descendants beyond number." Then Abraham waited patiently, and he received what God had promised (Heb. 6:13–15, NLT).

God had blessed them with the fruit of the womb as a reward for their great faith in Him.

Some years after this miraculous event, God suddenly made an unthinkable request. Abraham had been blessed with his long-awaited son, but now God asked him to offer the child up to Him as a burnt offering! What? We are about to witness how a true lover of God responds to Him when He appears to make an unthinkable and brutal request.

How could a loving God make such a cruel demand on Abraham, and would he obey such an outrageous command? What would he tell Sarah? What happens next is truly shocking, a rare lesson for all who desire to give God their over-the-top, mega love. Not only did Abraham obey God, but he did so promptly! After receiving God's command, Abraham loaded his donkey early the next morning and without hesitation set out on the three-day journey to the chosen location. He took his son Isaac, and two servants came along to assist him.

Abraham did not delay his obedience to God. He was prepared to worship God completely.

When he had cut enough wood for the burnt offering, he set out for the place God had told him about. On the third day Abraham looked up and saw the place in the distance. He said to his servants, "Stay here with the donkey while I and the boy go over there. We will worship and then we will come back to you. Abraham took the wood for the burnt offering and placed it on his son Isaac, and he himself carried the fire and the knife. As the two of them went on together, Isaac spoke up and said to his father Abraham, "Father?" "Yes, my son?" Abraham replied. "The fire and wood are here," Isaac said, "but where is the lamb for the burnt offering?" Abraham answered, "God himself will provide the lamb for the burnt offering, my son." And the two of them went on together. When they reached the place God had told him about, Abraham built an altar there and arranged the wood on it. He bound his son Isaac and laid him on the altar, on top of the wood. Then he reached out his hand and took the knife to slay his son. But the angel of the Lord called out to him from heaven, "Abraham! Abraham!" "Here I am," he replied. "Do not lay a hand on the boy," he said. "Do not do anything to him. Now I know that you fear God, because you have not withheld from me your son, your only son." Abraham looked up and there in a thicket he saw a ram caught by its horns. He went over and took the ram and sacrificed it as a burnt offering instead of his son. So Abraham called that place The Lord Will Provide. And to this day it is said, "On the mountain of the Lord it will be provided. The angel of the Lord called to Abraham from heaven a second time and said, "I swear by myself, declares the Lord, that because you have done this and have not withheld your son, your only son, I will surely bless you and make your descendants as numerous as the stars in the sky and as the sand on the seashore. Your descendants will take possession of the cities of their enemies, and through your offspring all nations on earth will be blessed, because you have obeyed me" (Gen 22:1–19, NIV).

We learn more of God's character and true nature through Abraham's excruciating submission. In a spectacular display of trust in God, regardless of the great pain it would have brought his family, Abraham completely obeyed God. He was willing to give up his long-awaited and miraculously conceived child as a sacrifice to demonstrate his uncommon love for God. We are given a glimpse into Abraham's reasoning in the book of Hebrews: "Abraham reasoned that if Isaac died, God was able to bring him back to life again. And in a sense, Abraham did receive his son back from the dead" (Heb. 11:19, NLT).

I am pretty sure I would not be willing to do this; I am not certain how you would respond. Abraham and Sarah give us a rare look into the depths of God's awesome power when He stopped the impending sacrifice of Isaac and provided Abraham with a ram instead. God blessed Abraham with the experience of receiving his son back from a virtual death sentence and left us an outstanding revelation of who He is: the resurrection and the life, and Jehovah Jireh (the God who provides).

If we are willing to submit completely to God, even when it looks as if we might suffer a great loss, we will encounter His spectacular and supernatural provision. He is the God who raises the dead! This event was a foretaste of things to come. God would later raise a widow's son; Lazarus, the brother of Mary and Martha; and a woman by the name of Tabitha. Ultimately God would give up His own only son as a sacrifice for the sins of all human beings when He raised Jesus Christ up from the dead. (See Luke 7:11–17, John 11:38–44, Acts 9:36–43, Hebrews 13:20.)

> For just as the Father raises the dead and gives them life, even so the Son gives life to whom he is pleased to give it (John 5:21, NIV).

> Jesus said to her, "I am the resurrection and the life. The one who believes in me will live, even though they die" (John 11:25, NIV).

We learn a great deal from the lives of believers who loved and trusted God completely. Without any exceptions, they all received amazing answers to their greatest needs. When we give God uncommon love and obedience, His ordained purpose will burst forth in our lives! The lesson to draw is this: God does not require brutal, excessive, or outlandish sacrifices from us to prove that we love Him. He just wants our full and total trust and obedience.

Uncommon blessings are released in lives that place their complete trust in God. Are you willing?

11

Where Is "All" the Love?
The Rich Young Ruler

I believe some verses from the gospel of Matthew will help us to hit the ground running on our quest to give God ultimate love. By applying these commandments from Jesus as our bedrock, we will swiftly unravel the answers to how each one of us can also give God our over-the-top, mega love. "Jesus replied, 'You must love the Lord your God with all your heart, all your soul, and all your mind. This is the first and greatest commandment'" (Matt. 22:37–38, NLT). This same commandment was given to Old Testament believers, not just to the New Testament followers of Jesus Christ. "And you must love the Lord your God with all your heart, all your soul, and all your strength" (Deut. 6:5, NLT).

According to these verses, those who desire to give God ultimate love must be prepared to do so with their whole hearts and entire beings. No halfhearted or low level of commitment will do when it comes to loving

God. If we genuinely desire to honor the Lord, our union with Him must be sincere and complete. No part of us can ever be withheld, concealed, or separated from Him. Our whole heart, soul, and strength will be fully involved if we are passionately pursuing God. This means putting God in first place. We need to love God with our all, above everyone and everything else.

These words are a great starting point, and if the response required to this commandment is correctly understood, our bond with God must be of the highest standard. The exhortation to love God with our whole hearts, souls, and strength is the basis for an authentic love union with Him. To further uncover the wisdom within these two verses, we need to take a quick look at the adjective *all* that is used to qualify how much of ourselves to yield to God. *All* is defined in the free dictionary as "everything, the whole quantity, every part, the (whole) lot, the entirety!"

And I hate to be the one to break this next bit of news to us. But *all* will include our money and assets. You might ask why our assets must be involved with loving God. *Because it's not all if it's not all.*

The most important relationship in our lives is the one we have with God. To love God more, we must treasure Him more. The scriptures inform us that human hearts become attached to their earthly treasures.

For where your treasure is, there your heart will be also (Matt. 6:21, BSB).

No one can serve two masters. For you will hate one and love the other; you will be devoted to one and despise the other. You cannot serve both God and money (Matt. 6:24, NLT).

If we desire to love God wholeheartedly, it is not possible to devote our whole heart to both Him and money or treasures at the same time. We will have to choose. When we place riches or wealth above God, they become idols to us, which makes a part of our hearts unavailable to love God. The story of a rich young ruler in the Bible will help us to understand and learn more about this. His life drives home the vital lesson that if we are unwilling to love God with our wealth and earthly possessions, then we are overly attached to our riches. We treasure them more than Him, and then we can love God only halfheartedly. Here is where the rubber really meets the road: if we want to give God over-the-top, mega love, we cannot be consumed with earthly things more than with Him.

Love originates from the heart, and we are exhorted to put everything into the right hierarchy in our lives. We need to remember that our lives and all our blessings come from God, the One who placed everyone and everything on the planet. God paves His heavenly streets with gold, so He is right to expect us to love Him more than gold, silver, or precious stones.

> Then I saw a new heaven and a new earth, for the old heaven and the old earth had disappeared. And the sea was also gone . . . . And the main street was pure gold, as clear as glass (Rev. 21:1, 21, NLT).

I am not suggesting that for us to please God we cannot enjoy our earthly possessions or the rewards we have worked so hard for. Nor do we have to reject any inheritances from loving parents or grandparents. We don't have to live in poverty to show that we love God. These words just remind us that wealth, riches, and assets are all gifts to us from God. He must come first in our hearts before them.

The gift giver is greater than the gift.

Treasuring the things we own more than the God who blessed us with them would be foolishness on our part. This would mean our hearts are not wholly available to Him, and the scriptures remind us not to exchange God's eternal treasures for temporary earthly ones.

> Do not store up for yourselves treasures on earth, where moth and rust destroy, and where thieves break in and steal. But store up for

yourselves treasures in heaven, where moth and rust do not destroy, and where thieves do not break in and steal (Matt. 6:19–20, BSB).

The rich young ruler I mentioned earlier believed he had obeyed God's laws from his youth. He was, however, reluctant to enter the fullness of God's grace when it came to loving God with His all. He was found wanting in this one area of his life during a brief, divine encounter with Jesus. A face-to-face meeting with God is a rare and ideal opportunity to correct any areas of our lives that are not in harmony with Him.

Then a certain ruler asked Him, "Good Teacher, what must I do to inherit eternal life?" "Why do you call Me good?" Jesus replied. "No one is good except God alone. You know the commandments: 'Do not commit adultery, do not murder, do not steal, do not bear false witness, honor your father and mother.'" "All these have I kept from my youth," he said. On hearing this, Jesus told him, "You still lack one thing: Sell everything you own and give to the poor, and you will have treasure in heaven. Then come, follow Me." But when the ruler heard this, he became very sad, because he was extremely wealthy(Luke 18:18–23, BSB).

Seriously! Did this young man just walk away from God's offer of eternal life in exchange for his wealth? He also separated himself from his true calling to follow God and directly violated the very first commandment God gave to Moses: "You must not have any other god but me" (Exod. 20:3, NLT).

This rich young ruler had been so sure he was living in full obedience to God's laws, yet he was unable to recognize this blind spot in his life. Seeing things through God's perspective will also reveal the blind spots in our own lives. The Bible helps us to fully understand the foolishness of some of the decisions we are about to make, and if God says "You still lack one thing," rest assured that you lack that one thing. The young man was not willing to let go of his possessions, so he let his great wealth come between him and God. This young man's wealth had become a great idol in his heart. By not letting go of his possessions as Jesus had instructed him, he gave up on God's offer of eternal life.

Neglecting to value the One who blessed us above all that we have is indeed great folly. Jesus is the way, truth, and life. Leaving all to follow Him is the same as embracing the fullest and best life, according to Jesus, who answered, "I am the way and the truth and the life. No one comes to the Father except through me" (John 14:6, NIV).

At the end of our lives we will have to leave behind all the wealth and possessions we spent our lives chasing and accumulating. Many of us will stand before God spiritually bankrupt, even though by earthly standards we might be very rich. We must never, ever allow this to happen! Loving God with our all must include our wealth and assets. If we are certain that God is the one doing the asking, we need to place our trust in Him and yield in obedience. It is important to note that we are *asked*. It is totally our choice. God does not grab anything from any one of us.

He owns everything. God's desire is to have our hearts. He is not after any of our possessions.

It is important to remember that whether it's a willing offering on our part, or an act of obedience to God's request, the choice to give a part or all of our wealth to God is always ours. There is no use of force on God's part; it is for whosoever will.

You must each decide in your heart how much to give. And don't give reluctantly or in response to pressure. "For God loves a person who gives cheerfully" (2 Cor. 9:7, NLT).

All must give as they are able, according to the blessings given to them by the LORD your God (Deut. 16:17, NLT).

For if the willingness is there, the gift is acceptable according to what one has, not according to what one does not have (2 Cor. 8:12, NIV).

We must choose whom we will follow—God or money. We cannot wholeheartedly follow both. I pray that when each of us faces this crucial choice in our own lives, that we will make the right decision. Our choices affect not only our lives but also the lives of our family members, communities, and, ultimately, nations. God will always respond to our generosity with abundant blessings. Sadly, the rich young man had already left Jesus. He did not trust enough in God's ability to provide for and bless him.

God's request to the rich young man to give his all to the poor was intended to help him free his heart from his over-attachment to stuff. Had he simply trusted in and obeyed God, his life and posterity would have been positively and eternally transformed. He missed the rarest of opportunities to honor God. Rejecting God's offer to exchange his temporary earthly treasures for enduring eternal ones was a most unwise choice by the young man. This was the worst decision of his life. We don't read any more about him in the scriptures and can only hope that he was given another opportunity to revisit this extremely poor choice. Had he stayed around and followed Jesus as commanded, he would have heard the following words: "'Truly I tell you,' Jesus replied, 'no one who has left home or wife or brothers or parents or children for the sake of the kingdom of God will fail to receive many times more at the proper time—and in the age to come, eternal life'" (Luke 18:29–30, BSB).

It is the ultimate blessing in life when God singles you out for a blessing. And if He gives you the special privilege of following and serving Him, you ought to do so right away! To borrow an expression, "You've just hit the greatest jackpot of your life!" God is the Creator of all that we possess. This commandment from Jesus to devote ourselves and our assets to God is intended to teach us that when we give our all to Him, He in return gives His all to us. And this exchange greatly favors us. It has often been said, "You cannot outgive God." May God deepen our understanding of His love and make us willing to yield ourselves and our all to Him. Ultimate love begins with loving God with an undivided heart, and true love for Him begins with faithful devotion. There are great blessings and awesome rewards stored up for those who will fully trust and obey God.

Trying to hold on to stuff more than to God is great folly. God rewards our trust in Him. We can have wealth and riches, but they must not have us.

The book of Proverbs also informs us that when we give generously to the poor there are tremendous blessings reserved for us by God. "If you help the poor, you are lending to the LORD—and he will repay you!" (Prov. 19:17, NLT). "One person gives freely, yet gains even more; another withholds unduly, but comes to poverty" (Prov. 11:24, NIV).

Whether it is a part or all our assets again, if we are confident that God is doing the asking, we must be wise enough to devote our "all" in obedience to Him. God will always exceed our expectations when He blesses us in return. We saw this principle at work in the life of King David. He was blessed with far more than we could ever give to God.

Do not be deceived: God is not mocked, for whatever one sows that will he also reap (Gal. 6:7, ESV).

And God will generously provide all you need. Then you will always have everything you need and plenty left over to share with others. As the scriptures say, "They share freely and give generously to the poor. Their good deeds will be remembered forever. For God is the one who provides seed for the farmer and then bread to eat. In the same way, he will provide and increase your resources and then produce a great harvest of generosity in you. Yes, you will be enriched in every way so that you can always be generous. And when we take your gifts to those who need them, they will thank God (2 Cor. 9:8–11, NIV).

Nothing you might ever have can come close to being blessed by God. Believers in both the Old and New Testaments embodied great generosity of their own free will by practicing giving as a joyful part of their worship. Without hesitation or pressure from any interested parties, they all freely gave of their assets to do the Lord's work. This made great wealth available to care for the needy among them. Whether a person was considered poor or rich, great or small, they all joined together in this beautiful unity of worship to love and honor God. Their love resulted in an outpouring of blessings from above, and this caused the good news of salvation to spread rapidly everywhere. The One to whom we are all giving ourselves is faithful. When we obey God without fear and submit ourselves wholly to Him, He will pour out blessings into our lives that will greatly surpass anything we could ever acquire on our own. "However, as it is written: 'What no eye has seen, what no ear has heard, and what no human mind has conceived'—the things God has prepared for those who love him" (1 Cor. 2:9, NIV).

Do you agree that ultimate love for God begins with enthusiastically loving Him with our all?

12

All of My Help Comes from God: The Poor Widow

The poor widow in the gospel of Mark is another great model for loving God and surrendering all to Him. Her actions were in clear contrast to the rich young ruler's actions, for this woman came to the temple prepared to give! Proceeding to demonstrate her great love and absolute trust in God, the widow placed all that she had left (two small copper coins) into the temple offering box. The small size and value of her gift indicates to us that the size or value of our gift does not matter to God because her coins were not worth that much. What matters is the heart from which our gift comes. She did not allow the poverty that typically accompanied widowhood then prevent her from showing her deep devotion to God. By giving Him her all, the woman was declaring through her actions that she fully trusted in God's ability to provide for her. The statement Jesus made after observing her tremendous sacrifice gives us fresh insight into God's perspective on trusting Him.

> As Jesus was sitting opposite the treasury, He watched the crowd placing money into it. And many rich people put in large amounts. Then one poor widow came and put in two small copper coins, which amounted to a small fraction of a denarius. Jesus called His disciples to Him and said, "Truly I tell you, this poor widow has put more than all the others into the treasury. For they all contributed out of their surplus, but she out of her poverty has put in all she had to live on" (Mark 12:41–44, BSB).

Based on God's word, we can be assured that these special words of commendation from Jesus were not all that she received from God. Her offering was an outstanding example of extravagant love and extreme submission in worship. Her attitude was a complete antithesis to the rich young ruler's when he was challenged to surrender his all to and trust completely in God. Obedience to God in every area of our lives necessitates fully trusting Him. The poor widow demonstrated her faith in God when she surrendered all to Him. God promises to bless us with pressed-down, shaken-together, making-room-for-more, running-over, and poured-into-our-laps rewards for our generosity toward Him.

> Give, and you will receive. Your gift will return to you in full—pressed down, shaken together to make room for more, running over, and poured into your lap. The amount you give will determine the amount you get back (Luke 6:38, NLT).

> Remember this: Whoever sows sparingly will also reap sparingly, and whoever sows generously will also reap generously" (2 Cor. 9:6, NIV).

When we give to God, we demonstrate our love for and trust in Him. God is the only one with an eternal supply of everything we need. It was a wise move on the widow's part to entrust herself completely to God, because by transferring what could not sustain her in the long term into the hands of Jehovah Jireh (the God who provides), her little became much. Her meager resources became consecrated when she connected them to God, and He could now take over the full responsibility of providing for her. God could now also greatly multiply what she had entrusted to Him, because God responds to our faith with extravagant blessings in extraordinary ways. He blesses us back with far more than we can ever give to Him, and the most important lesson to draw from this woman's example is this: rich or poor, those who love truly are generous givers!

At this point we need to take a deep breath and remind ourselves that we don't need to depend solely on our own willpower or determination to love or please God in any way. All our help comes from the Lord, and every new move of God begins with God. If we simplify our lives and yield ourselves to God, then we allow Him to accomplish His purpose in and through us. We can do nothing solely with our own strength; we need to align ourselves with God's word. We learned earlier that we cannot genuinely learn to love others without first receiving love from God: "My help comes from the LORD, who made heaven and earth!" (Ps. 121:2, NLT). "May the grace of the Lord Jesus Christ, the love of God, and the fellowship of the Holy Spirit be with you all" (2 Cor. 13:14, NLT).

When we rely on and draw from His strength, we receive the necessary grace to do His bidding. This takes all the pressure off us. When we remember that He is the one who strengthens and makes us willing and able to accomplish what pleases Him, then we don't have to be panicked or depressed about fulfilling what might seem like a very tall order.

It all came together for me one Sunday afternoon during our church worship service: you cannot love anyone with your whole heart, soul, mind, and assets unless you're passionately in love with him! I recently watched a skit that perfectly illustrated the point that genuine love is all or nothing. Imagine an excited young man proposing to his fiancée on bended knee. She was the love of his life, and he was asking her to marry him. The young woman, equally excited, said *"Yes!"* adding with great joy that they would be so happy together and how devoted to him she was. She promised to date other men from then on only for one week in every leap year! I mean, she gave their relationship top priority, right? Except for the extremely rare occasions when she would see other men. That shouldn't have been too much to ask since she would have been spending most of her time with her husband, so that makes things right, doesn't it? That's quite the commitment to love, isn't it? I wonder how many of us would accept such a ridiculous proposal.

Our love for and faithful commitment to God should be of no lesser quality than the one we make to a fellow human. In fact, it should be a much stronger bond.

Nothing and no one should ever come between us and God. We don't get married with the full intention of cheating on our spouses, nor are we supposed to neglect them or place anyone else above them. Why do we think this is all right when it comes to loving God? Marriage is a commitment to love one another exclusively for a lifetime because we've found that very special one to build a family with. What a wonderful relief it is to know that God's Holy Spirit living on the inside of us is fully responsible for pouring God's love into our hearts. We don't have to pretend to have affection for God or others that we do not possess.

For we know how dearly God loves us, because he has given us the Holy Spirit to fill our hearts with his love (Rom. 5:5, NLT).

And because we are his children, God has sent the Spirit of his Son into our hearts, prompting us to call out, "Abba, Father" (Gal. 4:6, NLT).

We can simply plug into and draw from the true source of life and love: God. When we understand how much God loves us and all He has done to save and keep us in His family, then we will find it easier to give Him our wholehearted love. His love also makes us able to faithfully love our spouses and others through grace. Israel's King David again is a great example for relying on God for all our help. He prayed the following prayer seeking God's help to be able to love Him wholeheartedly. David did not try to do things in his own strength or with his own will power:

Teach me your way, LORD, that I may rely on your faithfulness; give me an undivided heart, that I may fear your name. I will praise you, Lord my God, with all my heart; I will glorify your name forever. For great is your love toward me (Ps. 86:11–13, NIV).

When we submit to God, we are submitting to true *agape* love. God will, in return, enable us to enjoy and participate in the world around us at a whole new level. The way to savor life is to abide in God's love. We need to align our hearts to His word, and we don't have to dwell on any past mistakes or keep looking back to try to make up for lost time. The grace that we need to live a blessed and fruitful life daily comes from God. "We do this by keeping our eyes on Jesus, the champion who initiates and perfects our faith" (Heb. 12:2, NLT).

Pray and seek the Lord for His help and the grace to be a faithful lover.

13

No Pressure,
There's More!

As we go further with our topic, we find another commandment from Jesus that will help us unlock what ultimate love for God is all about. Jesus paints an intensely passionate picture of a true disciple in the following words: "If you want to be my disciple, you must hate everyone else by comparison—your father and mother, wife and children, brothers and sisters—yes, even your own life. Otherwise, you cannot be my disciple" (Luke 14:26, NLT).

Of all the commandments about loving God, this may be the most difficult one to wrap our hearts and heads around. Is God really saying we must completely let go of all other people and things and put Him in first place always? If this is so, is that realistic? To answer this, it is vitally important to state that God is not asking us to love Him with our whole hearts and entire beings and put Him first because He is on an ego trip.

He does not need our love to make Him feel important, nor does He require our worship to prop Him up on His throne. God has no equal, He is the Supreme Being. He needs no one and no things from us to support or sustain Him. The eternal, self-existing God is omniscient, omnipotent, and omnipresent. He is complete within Himself. So what was Jesus saying? He was simply enlightening us on a most significant point: we need to devote ourselves wholly to God for our sakes, not His. With every fiber of our being, we need God.

More than anyone or anything else, we are the ones who desperately need God. Everything we are and own comes directly from Him. Our devotion to God must be of the highest quality—the ultimate. As He tried to do with the rich young ruler, Jesus was teaching His disciples that whenever we prioritize other relationships, activities, and things above God, it behooves us to remember that we totally depend upon Him. Humankind owes its entire existence and all that we have to God. We may not always acknowledge this, but God is the only one who truly deserves our ultimate devotion in every way. And we need His love, protection, guidance, and provision before we need anyone else's or anything else on the earth.

Giving God our all is not just about demonstrating our love for Him; it is also a serious reminder that to live fully productive lives, we must stay connected to God. We can be, have, and produce nothing without Him, because our lives depend completely on God.

Yes, I am the vine; you are the branches. Those who remain in me, and I in them, will produce much fruit. For apart from me you can do nothing (John 15:5, NLT).

For in him we live and move and exist. As some of your own poets have said, "We are his offspring" (Acts 17:28, NLT).

We cannot stay alive, blossom, or flourish apart from God. Repenting from our sins, receiving His forgiveness, and loving Him with our whole hearts form the foundation for truly abundant living. We need to go after God with our whole hearts because love is an all-or-nothing venture. God wants us in His family, but we need Him for our entire existences.

When a man falls in love, he goes after the woman he wants with his whole heart. His other relationships take a backseat as he pursues his beloved, and he won't relent till he secures her love. I recall once hearing the wife of a past presidential candidate recount the moment she realized how much she meant to the young man she had been dating. He had gone away on a long trip and upon his return, his girlfriend and family were waiting eagerly to meet him. The telling moment was when the young man got out of the car, ran past his mother, and fell into the arms of his then girlfriend! They got married.

Jesus again makes it plain not only that our hearts, minds, and assets will be involved in this greatest love of all, but also that our most cherished relationships must be relegated to their rightful second place after God.

Again, I emphasize that this is not meant to pressure us or force us to devote ourselves to God. And we must remember that all we bring to God was first created by and received from Him. In reality, we are only returning to Him a tiny portion of what we have first received from Him. All these are simply our way of connecting our lives to and honoring God. Wonderful blessings are in store for all who truly love and commit themselves wholly to God. He is the one from whom all blessings flow, and loving God wholeheartedly is the bedrock for a love union with Him.

These two major commandments serve as solid foundations for our relationship with God. Whether we are aware of or choose to show gratitude to God or not, everyone on our planet desperately needs God. We must embrace this truth and be willing to love Him back with our lives, assets, gifts, and relationships. We have no life, relationships, responsibilities, or any other preoccupations if God does not first grant them to us. Obeying His commands may appear burdensome, but this is not at all so. Realigning our hearts and priorities with God's word will help us to become all that He has destined for us to be. This can only be done through God's enabling grace.

We will learn more later about the promised rewards for those who keep God first in their lives. But without delay, we need to make the decision to heal our broken connection with God and strengthen our union with Him. Jesus' words remind us that the need to love God extravagantly is ours and that we need to put Him in first place to enter into the highest dimension of living.

Love springs from sincere hearts that are rightfully connected to God. We may want to argue that we are too busy to put God first all the time. Many of our pursuits are legitimate, obligatory tasks that need our focus, and various relationships and activities vie daily for our attention. Different competing interests require our full participation, and for survival on our planet our duties seem endless! We have tons of responsibilities needing our attention, and to be fully productive in our world, we need to do many things.

In light of all these facts, how can anyone realistically put God first all the time? How do we elevate loving God above so many people and things? This mission appears to be impossible! Are you feeling tempted to give up on the idea of loving God with your all? After we acknowledge our feelings, this truth still remains: without God we have no life. For our own sakes, we must restore God to His rightful first place in our hearts. We cannot fully enjoy and participate in all that life has to offer without first learning to love God. If we truly desire to give God ultimate love, He must be our first priority.

We must then stay closely connected to Him in the midst of our busy lives, giving our hearts wholly to Him.

The need to stay connected to God daily is ours and not His.

Let's continue to seek after and commit ourselves to God by obeying Him and giving Him our love with everything we've got! The closer our walk with God is, the more skillfully He can work through our other relationships and activities to keep us in harmony with Him. Our lives really become new when God is placed on the throne of our hearts as our most beloved one. "Therefore, if anyone is in Christ, the new creation has come: The old has gone, the new is here!" (2 Cor. 5:17, NIV).

In light of the examples we've seen already, are you ready to take things up several notches when it comes to loving God?

14

Successful Leaders Love God with Their All: Deborah and Anna

Two courageous women will also be of great value in our study. Both these women loved God so dearly that they gave themselves completely to Him. One of them was a married woman, while the other one was not. This tells us that our status, whether married or single, does not prevent us from loving and serving God with our all. We begin with Deborah, who lived during the period of the judges, a time of great turmoil in the nation of Israel. Because they had cast aside God's word and decided to go their own way, the people were suffering greatly under the tyranny of their enemies. See Judges 3:5, 7-8. The safety and wellbeing of every citizen in the nation were severely threatened, and there was also a vacuum in their leadership. This state of rebellion would require a very strong leader, and God chose a woman named Deborah to do the job.

The task ahead of her was a formidable one, and she would need to hear God's voice clearly to restore the knowledge of God throughout the land. Leading her people out of oppression would be no small job, and putting the entire nation back on the right track would require a very brave leader. Deborah needed to secure victory for her people, and only by living in complete submission to God could she receive His divine wisdom. She had been placed on a platform of such great national prominence during these patriarchal times that her mission could be successfully accomplished only through God's grace.

Again the Israelites did evil in the eyes of the Lord, now that Ehud was dead. So the Lord sold them into the hands of Jabin king of Canaan, who reigned in Hazor. Sisera, the commander of his army, was based in Harosheth Haggoyim. Because he had nine hundred chariots fitted with iron and had cruelly oppressed the Israelites for twenty years, they cried to the Lord for help. Now Deborah, a prophet, the wife of Lappidoth, was leading Israel at that time. She held court under the Palm of Deborah between Ramah and Bethel in the hill country of Ephraim, and the Israelites went up to her to have their disputes decided (Judg. 4:1–6, NIV).

Occupying the highest position of leadership as Israel's prophetic leader, Deborah had been entrusted with delivering God's people from their sufferings. This would require great courage on her part. God had chosen Deborah to rescue her nation, and her commitment to God had to be unbreakable. Israel had endured many years of severe hardships, and appointing Deborah as prophetess and judge over them was God's solution, because He had decided to have compassion on them. She presided over His people on God's behalf, and everyone in Israel, great or small, brought all their cases to Deborah.

This prophetic leader had received a true calling from God and shared God's Word with His people after first receiving it from Him. This woman of great faith would also find herself accompanying the nation's military leaders into battle against their enemies, the Canaanites.

She sent for Barak son of Abinoam from Kedesh in Naphtali and said to him, "The Lord, the God of Israel, commands you: 'Go, take with you ten thousand men of Naphtali and Zebulun and lead them up to Mount Tabor. I will lead Sisera, the commander of Jabin's army, with his chariots and his troops to the Kishon River and give him into your hands.'" Barak said to her, "If you go with me, I will go; but if you don't go with me, I won't go." "Certainly I will go with you," said Deborah. "But because of the course you are taking, the honor will not be yours, for the LORD will deliver Sisera into the hands of a woman." So Deborah went with Barak to Kedesh. There Barak summoned Zebulun and Naphtali, and ten thousand men went up under his command. Deborah also went up with him . . . . Then Deborah said to Barak, "Go! This is the day the LORD has given Sisera into your hands. Has not the LORD gone ahead of you?" So Barak went down Mount Tabor, with ten thousand men following him. At Barak's advance, the LORD routed Sisera and all his chariots and army by the sword, and Sisera got down from his chariot and fled on foot. Barak pursued the chariots and army as far as Harosheth Haggoyim, and all Sisera's troops fell by the sword; not a man was left (Judg. 4:6–10, 14–16, NIV).

Spending quality time in God's presence is the prerequisite to success in all that we try to do for Him. We must also add that Deborah was the wife of a man by the name of Lappidoth, so she needed to carefully balance her God-given duties with her domestic life. To serve God and her family well and for everything in her life to go smoothly, she would need clear guidance and precise instructions from the Lord. That meant abiding daily in God's presence.

We learn from another of Israel's leaders, the prophet Samuel, that successful leadership could be achieved only when the leader prioritized spending time with God. Samuel heard clearly from and was fully obedient to God. This made him victorious in all his ways because God was with him.

The boy Samuel ministered before the LORD under Eli. In those days the word of the LORD was rare; there were not many visions (1 Sam. 3:1, NIV).

The LORD came and stood there, calling as at the other times, "Samuel! Samuel!" Then Samuel said, "Speak, for your servant is listening" (1 Sam. 3:10, NIV).

And Samuel grew, and the LORD was with him, and He let none of Samuel's words fall to the ground. So all Israel from Dan to Beersheba knew that Samuel was confirmed as a prophet of the LORD. And the LORD continued to appear at Shiloh, because there He revealed Himself to Samuel by His word (1 Sam. 3:19–21, BSB).

The leader before Samuel was a priest named Eli, who failed to honor and obey God. He totally disregarded spending time in God's presence, which led to the destruction of his family and Israel's defeat in battle.

> The man who brought the news replied, "Israel
> fled before the Philistines, and the army has suf-
> fered heavy losses. Also your two sons, Hophni
> and Phinehas, are dead, and the ark of God has
> been captured." When he mentioned the ark of
> God, Eli fell backward off his chair by the side
> of the gate. His neck was broken and he died (1
> Sam. 4:17–18, NIV).

Failure was not an option for Deborah and her
nation during such perilous times, and the nation was
counting on her successful leadership. The daily rigors
of being a national leader required nothing less than the
wisdom that comes directly from God. Deborah's access
to God's counsel came as a direct result of spending
quality time in His presence, and her successful leadership gave Israel rest from their enemies for another forty
years. From the song of praise she sang to God after the
nation's victory over their enemies, we are able to catch a
glimpse of Deborah's walk with God.

> On that day Deborah and Barak son of Abi-
> noam sang this song: "When the princes in
> Israel take the lead, when the people willingly
> offer themselves—praise the LORD! Hear this,
> you kings! Listen, you rulers! I, even I, will sing

to the LORD; I will praise the LORD, the God
of Israel, in song . . . . The highways were abandoned; travelers took to winding paths. Vil-
lagers in Israel would not fight; they held back
until I, Deborah, arose, until I arose, a mother
in Israel . . . . So may all your enemies perish,
LORD! But may all who love you be like the sun
when it rises in its strength. Then the land had
peace forty years" (Judg. 5:1–3, 6–7, 31, NIV).

Deborah excelled as a result of her love for God, and her
success was entirely due to her close union with Him. Will
you begin to prioritize time alone with God?

Anna's Mega Love: A Different Type of Warfare

Another example of devotion to and exemplary love of
God is seen in the life of an awesome woman named
Anna. She was widowed at a very young age but decided
to spend the rest of her life serving God in the temple.
Instead of getting married again, she worshipped and
prayed to Him daily, just like the prophet Samuel. She
ministered to God by spending quality time in His presence. Her quiet, low-key style of serving God proves
that we can all serve God in whatever capacity we find
ourselves. Although women were not allowed to be
priests during her time, Anna's leadership as interces-
sor and spiritual warfare leader for her people cannot be

disregarded. Unlike her married forerunner Deborah, Anna was widowed but was also called and anointed by God to be a prophetess. This devoted prayer warrior and prophetic servant leader set a powerful example of service to God. She was one of the first to recognize Jesus as the Savior and Redeemer of humankind when his parents brought Him to the temple to be dedicated to God. Anna spoke about Him to all who came to worship God, and her name is recorded in the New Testament for all generations after her. (See Luke 2:36–38.)

Her style was completely different from that of Deborah. While Deborah had to project strength and march into battle with the nation's military leaders, Anna was a much older woman who led God's people in a very different type of warfare. Through her persistent prayers, she led the nation in spiritual warfare until God's promised Savior for the nation and the entire world could appear. This task was successfully accomplished by Anna.

We are all perfect for our purposes. There is room for everyone to serve God through our different personalities and life circumstances.

She worshipped God day and night with fasting and prayers and never left God's house, the temple. Again we observe that the key to achieving great success is how much time we spend in God's presence. This mature woman fulfilled her calling in a subtler way than Deborah did, yet both women enjoyed great fruitfulness in their labors for the Lord. They were both true to their callings, and each one set an example of ultimate love for God in her own unique way.

We must commit to loving God wholeheartedly regardless of our status in life. Anna's quiet and enduring spiritual discipline gave her unrivalled prophetic insight into God's plan of salvation for her nation and all humankind. Anna's role as a prophet was also one of the five types of leadership God gave to the church after Jesus' resurrection and ascension.

> And the same one who descended is the one who ascended higher than all the heavens, so that he might fill the entire universe with himself. Now these are the gifts Christ gave to the church: the apostles, the prophets, the evangelists, and the pastors and teachers. Their responsibility is to equip God's people to do his work and build up the church, the body of Christ. This will continue until we all come to such unity in our faith and knowledge of God's Son that we will be mature in the Lord, measuring up to the full and complete standard of Christ (Eph. 4:10–13, NLT).

When we walk in total reverence and love for God, we become vessels through which He can restore broken lives. Anna demonstrated her reliance on God by making Him the ultimate love of her life after her husband passed away.

Will we continue to love God wholeheartedly regardless of our status in life?

15

Mary's "Yes" to God Paved the Way for Us All

Mary, the mother of Jesus, also displayed great love for God by serving Him in her own unique way. She left us an outstanding example of giving God our all, and in my first book, *I Made It Through*, I share some relevant observations about her life. The lessons we can learn from this young woman when she faced a sudden encounter with an angel are still important today. God's special messenger appeared suddenly to Mary and announced that she would be the special vessel chosen to give birth to the Son of God—Jesus!

Her response to this extremely shocking news is a classic model for all who desire to give God their ultimate love. The sudden brief encounter was something no one could be coached or prepared for ahead of time, but Mary responded without hesitation. Like other great devotees of God before her, she instantly surrendered herself fully to God, giving her complete submission to

Him. Mary did not run home to first seek her parents' counsel, nor did she rush to the synagogue for her rabbi's prayers. This is most impressive when you also consider that she was a very young teenager at that time. Her immediate complete submission was an unrehearsed reaction to the divine interruption of her life. This is truly awe-inspiring!

> "Don't be afraid, Mary," the angel told her, "for you have found favor with God! You will conceive and give birth to a son, and you will name him Jesus. He will be very great and will be called the Son of the Most High. The Lord God will give him the throne of his ancestor David. And he will reign over Israel forever; his Kingdom will never end!" Mary asked the angel, "But how can this happen? I am a virgin." The angel replied, "The Holy Spirit will come upon you, and the power of the Most High will overshadow you. So the baby to be born will be holy, and he will be called the Son of God. For nothing is impossible with God." Mary responded, "I am the Lord's servant. May everything you have said about me come true." And then the angel left her (Luke 1:30–35, 37–38, NLT).

This young woman found herself in a situation no one could ever imagine, but when her ordinary life was turned completely upside down by God, she was willing to obey. Her instant "yes" to God is the key that shows how faith releases God's power within us. Mary displayed genuine humility and ultimate trust in God when she was selected to be the very special woman to give birth to humankind's deliverer. Mary would be the mother of the Savior of the world.

Mary's spontaneous and unhesitant reaction revealed that her heart completely trusted in God.

The message she received from God also appeared to nullify her engagement to the man she loved, Joseph, but Mary's solid faith in Him is truly impressive. She would need to continue relying completely on God as she encountered multiple challenges, including a great escape to Egypt with her new family. (See Matt. 2:13–14.) Things ultimately came to a head in Mary's life when she had to cast herself entirely upon God's grace after the traumatic loss of her miraculously conceived son on a cross for crimes He had not committed. Her completely unshakeable submission to God reflected a lifestyle of total devotion to Him, and from her obedience we capture the full picture of Mary's love for God.

Mary, a quiet, humble, servant leader, lived in full surrender to God, though she held no other special title or position except mother. Her obedience to God paved the way of salvation for our entire planet.

Our observations are confirmed in the song of praise Mary sang to God after the supernatural conception of her first child and all the amazing events in her life.

And Mary said, "My soul magnifies the Lord, and my spirit rejoices in God my Savior, for he has looked on the humble estate of his servant. For behold, from now on all generations will call me blessed: for he who is mighty has done great things for me, and holy is his name. And his mercy is for those who fear him from generation to generation. He has shown strength with his arm; he has scattered the proud in the thoughts of their hearts; he has brought down the mighty from their thrones and exalted those of humble estate; he has filled the hungry with good things, and the rich he has sent away empty. He has helped his servant Israel, in remembrance of his mercy, as he spoke to our fathers, to Abraham and to his offspring forever (Luke 1:46–55, ESV).

Mary was prepared for her destiny by God, and she endured a myriad of trials while obeying Him. She left us a snapshot of one woman's mega love for God.

Will you be willing to accept God's call to do great things even if it means not holding any special titles or positions as Mary did?

16

Sacrificial Worship Brings Deliverance: Paul and Silas

To give God ultimate love, we also need to be devoted to Him during challenging times in our lives. If things become too difficult for us to handle, will we continue loving God? Or do we love Him only when things are going well for us? While it may look like He sometimes allows His children to suffer persecution or go through severe pain, we must learn to trust Him because His nature is love. Despite negative circumstances, we must place a high priority on being in God's presence so that His anointing power can be released upon our lives. His mighty power moves on our behalf when we continue to honor and trust Him even during difficult times. This will inevitably affect our circumstances for the better.

Two missionaries, Paul and Silas, demonstrated their solid, childlike trust in God despite facing great adversity. They valued their connection with God and did not allow their dire circumstances to interrupt their worship. Their unshakeable trust in God yielded so much fruit for God's kingdom that they give us another great model to follow. These two servants of God teach us valuable lessons about giving God our sacrificial worship during difficult times.

Paul was born in the city of Tarsus as a Pharisee of the highest pedigree, and his parents originally named him Saul. At first, this young man sincerely believed that the good news of salvation through Jesus Christ was a heresy. As far as he was concerned, the gospel message was contrary to the established Jewish traditions of his day. Being a bona fide Pharisee, he considered it his religious duty to persecute and imprison Christians wherever they were found. Saul was on his way to Damascus one day to enforce Jewish law when he had a miraculous encounter with the Lord Jesus Christ. The experience completely transformed his life and led this fervent advocate of persecuting and killing Christians to instantly become a follower of Jesus Christ.

Although he had previously been one of its strongest critics, he became Christianity's strongest advocate. After God saved him in this way, Paul was baptized in water (Acts 9:1–6) and had his name changed from Saul to Paul (Acts 13:9). Paul lived the rest of his life serving

God and wrote many of the books of the New Testament. Right after his conversion, he began to travel and share the good news of salvation through Jesus Christ, telling people what God had done for him. He soon became the target of the same sort of persecution he had formerly participated in and would suffer greatly for his faith. Often severely beaten and imprisoned many times, this fervent believer in Christ did not let the extreme persecution he had to withstand prevent him from following and serving God. He counted the life he had lived before as garbage, and continued to be one of Christianity's strongest servants.

> Yes, everything else is worthless when compared with the infinite value of knowing Christ Jesus my Lord. For his sake I have discarded everything else, counting it all as garbage, so that I could gain Christ (Phil. 3:8, NLT).

> For to me, to live is Christ and to die is gain (Phil. 1:21, NIV).

Paul often went on missionary journeys and traveled through different regions to spread the good news of salvation through Jesus Christ. He founded churches in the cities he visited and appointed elders over each congregation. The New Testament books attributed to him were written as letters to those new churches, and as laborers with God in His great plan of restoration, we can learn a great deal from Paul's example of endurance and steadfastness. In the face of multiple adversities and grueling sufferings, he is a rare example of ultimate love for God.

Paul never faltered in his faith, regardless of the tribulations he had to endure. He was often in danger and occasionally near death, but he continued to share the good news about Jesus with the lost. He fully participated in God's vast mission to rescue His lost children by taking full responsibility for the new converts he led to the Lord. Paul fervently served God despite seemingly never-ending hardships. His enthusiasm and unwavering commitment to God are captured in the following verses.

> Not only so, but we also glory in our sufferings, because we know that suffering produces perseverance (Rom. 5:3, NIV).

> We are pressed on all sides, but not crushed; perplexed, but not in despair; persecuted, but not forsaken; struck down, but not destroyed. We always carry around in our body the death of Jesus, so that the life of Jesus may also be revealed in our body (2 Cor. 4:8–10, BSB).

> That is why, for Christ's sake, I delight in weaknesses, in insults, in hardships, in persecutions,

in difficulties. For when I am weak, then I am strong (2 Cor. 12:10, NIV).

We do not want you to be uninformed, brothers and sisters, about the troubles we experienced in the province of Asia. We were under great pressure, far beyond our ability to endure, so that we despaired of life itself (2 Cor. 1:8, NIV).

Five times I received from the Jews the forty lashes minus one. Three times I was beaten with rods, once I was stoned, three times I was shipwrecked. I spent a night and a day in the open sea. In my frequent journeys, I have been in danger from rivers and from bandits, in danger from my countrymen and from the Gentiles, in danger in the city and in the country, in danger on the sea and among false brothers. In labor and toil and often without sleep, in hunger and thirst and often without food, in cold and exposure. Apart from these external trials, I face daily the pressure of my concern for all the churches. Who is weak, and I am not weak? Who is led into sin, and I do not burn with grief? (2 Cor. 11:24–29, BSB).

Paul's attitude toward his sufferings was also powerfully illustrated in an encounter he had on one of his missionary journeys. While traveling with his Christian companion Silas, the two came across a female slave possessed by a very foul spirit (a python spirit) and set her free. The evil spirit gave the woman supernatural abilities of fortune telling, and her special abilities brought great wealth to her owners. After being set free, she lost all her special powers, and all the revenue she had brought for her owners was lost. The slave owners were furious and retaliated against Paul and Silas by severely flogging them and throwing them into prison. This severe attack did not stop the two men from giving God their enthusiastic praises and worship at midnight! Although the slave owners had unleashed their great fury against Paul and Silas, the two responded to their hardship with love toward God expressed through their worship. Although they were in tremendous pain, they did not cease giving thanks to God in the midst of these horrible circumstances. They both displayed a depth of love for God that is truly worthy of emulation.

> They brought them to the magistrates and said, "These men are Jews and are throwing our city into turmoil by promoting customs that are unlawful for us Romans to adopt or practice." The crowd joined in the attack against Paul and Silas, and the magistrates ordered that they be stripped and beaten with rods. And after striking them with many blows, they

threw them into prison and ordered the jailer to guard them securely. On receiving this order, he placed them in the inner cell and fastened their feet in the stocks. About midnight, Paul and Silas were praying and singing hymns to God, and the other prisoners were listening to them. Suddenly a strong earthquake shook the foundations of the prison. At once all the doors flew open, and everyone's chains came loose. When the jailer woke up and saw the prison doors open, he drew his sword and was about to kill himself, presuming that the prisoners had escaped. But Paul called out in a loud voice, "Do not harm yourself! We are all here!" Calling for lights, the jailer rushed in and fell trembling before Paul and Silas. Then he brought them out and asked, "Sirs, what must I do to be saved?" They replied, "Believe in the Lord Jesus and you will be saved, you and your household." Then Paul and Silas spoke the word of the Lord to him and to everyone in his house. At that hour of the night, the jailer took them and washed their wounds. And without delay, he and all his household were baptized (Acts 16:21–33, BSB).

Paul and Silas did not change sides. They offered God adoration and praises by delighting in Him despite being locked up in chains. Their crimes were preaching about Jesus and setting the captives free, and they taught by their powerful example that we should continue loving and honoring God regardless of our circumstances in life. The depth of love they demonstrated toward God shows us that we should not let our faith in God diminish even during tremendous trials. Their sacrificial worship resulted in great deliverance when God's power was released in the prison where they were being held captive. God responded to Paul and Silas' praises with a mighty earthquake and publicly removed their chains!

All these things came to pass as a direct result of their faithfulness toward God. The two missionaries had remained steadfast in their faith in the midst of adversity, and everyone—including their jailer—experienced a mighty move of God. This spectacular supernatural outpouring of God's power transformed their terrible circumstances, and everyone in prison with them was also set free from their chains! When we honor God during difficult times, we make room for His miraculous interventions.

While we don't always understand why we are in certain circumstances, if we will stay loyal to God, He grants us the grace to endure and overcome. Even though they faced the real threat of death, Paul and Silas' worship of God did not cease. Multiple miracles transpired, and the jailer and his entire family turned to God in genuine repentance that same night. They humbled themselves and received God's free pardon. Salvation came to all of these people because two missionaries acted as powerful witnesses for the Lord. The power everyone witnessed was incontrovertible evidence that the gospel message preached by Paul and Silas was true.

God causes the outcome of our trials to be for our good and His glory. Our suffering is never in vain. When we surrender all to God, we are never disappointed by Him.

In the midst of all the suffering in our world today, people may not understand the wisdom behind giving God worship during difficult times. A true worshipper's response to pain might be at odds with general convention. We must not allow this to deter us from giving God our ultimate love. Even when we go through excruciating circumstances, we see from these two disciples of God that when a true worshipper faces adversity, the correct response must be a rock-solid faith in God.

Paul and Silas sang praises to God at midnight, and their enemies were completely silenced by Him. The message of the gospel was affirmed by God's awesome power, and by daybreak, Paul and Silas' faith had prevailed over evil. Their victory produced so many blessings for the kingdom of God that we still refer to it today. We mature as worshippers when we trust God completely, and if we can glorify God in the most difficult moments of our lives, this creates an opportunity for an even greater witness about His grace. Trusting God with our entire beings at all times is one of the greatest treasures we can give to Him. It is a sacrifice of praise! And giving God our ultimate love does not depend upon our circumstances but upon our commitment to Him.

It is easy to give God praise when things are going smoothly, but what will your response be if the opposite becomes true?

17

Ultimate Trust in God Yields Ultimate Fruit: Hannah

Two women in the Bible, Hannah and Elizabeth, will also help us to learn a great deal about loving God. They were both married, and their husbands shared their great reverence for God. But despite their faithful devotion, both couples were barren. It appeared that one of life's most significant blessings was about elude them. How would their faith be affected by these trials, and how did these two couples handle their barrenness? Would their negative circumstances extinguish their love for God? Or would they remain faithful to Him in spite of what looked like unanswered prayers? Let's find out.

When you also consider the blessings promised to all who delight themselves in God, you would think that these two devout couples deserved His blessings. But although they sought Him fervently with prayers for

many years, their barrenness persisted. It is also noteworthy that barrenness in those days was an awful stigma.
It was regarded as a curse or even a punishment from
God for sin in a person's life, a clear mark of disgrace.
(See Exodus 23:26 and Deuteronomy 7:14.) So for these
devout believers, it would have been doubly painful to
be perceived as people with whom God was not pleased.

What lessons can we learn from them that will help
to illustrate how we are to respond to God in the midst of
life's negative circumstances? Let's begin with Hannah.
Hannah was a devout worshipper whose inability to bear
children put her in a complex situation with her husband
Elkanah. He dearly loved Hannah, but her barrenness
led him to take a second wife to bear him children. This
was the custom in their day, and Elkanah had chosen a
young woman named Peninnah. And though she was a
very fertile young woman, Peninnah was very cruel. She
would taunt Hannah every day, mocking her until she
cried and lost her appetite.

Year after year this went on, and Peninnah gave
birth to one child after another. She grew bolder and
colder at ridiculing Hannah with each new birth and
also showed her irreverence toward God by displaying
this detestable behavior when the family went up to
worship during their pilgrimage to a large festival held
yearly. At the temple in Shiloh, Hannah got no rest from
her rival. The sacred celebrations did not deter Peninnah
from making Hannah's life miserable. This unsolicited

rivalry was a source of constant anguish for this woman, but she is about to teach us some awe-inspiring lessons. (See 1 Samuel 1:1–8.)

Although her negative circumstances severely tested Hannah's faith, she continued to love and faithfully seek God. Our lessons begin with the tremendous example of forbearance and fortitude she displayed while withstanding daily insults from her self-proclaimed rival. Hannah did not allow her barrenness to diminish her trust in God, and her persistent faith and passionate prayers to Him never ceased. Although it seemed like her prayers were unanswered, Hannah did not abandon her faith but instead cast herself entirely upon God's mercy. She let her deep anguish motivate her to seek the Lord more.

Responding to her difficult circumstances with outstanding faith, despite what looked like unmet expectations from God, Hannah did not allow her circumstances to negatively affect her love for God. You will recall that earlier in this study, we saw that giving God our all is the bedrock for an authentic union with Him. Hannah, however, is about to introduce us to a never-before-seen or -heard-of level of trusting God. She decided to devote not only all that she already possessed to God, but also all that she hoped to receive from Him in the future! During one of the family's yearly visits to the temple in Shiloh, things turned around radically for Hannah when she decided to intensify her prayers and take her faith to a whole new level of trust in God.

In a stunning move, Hannah surrendered herself to God with ultimate trust in His love and ability to deliver her, by exercising *crazy faith!* She dedicated a yet-to-be-conceived child to the Lord's service, and although God had seemed oblivious to her predicament, Hannah's move revealed that this was not at all the case. Hannah's ultimate trust in God was on full display, and she gave us a sterling example of what faith in God is all about. Again, you can't outgive God.

> Once when they had finished eating and drinking in Shiloh, Hannah stood up. Now Eli the priest was sitting on his chair by the doorpost of the Lord's house. In her deep anguish Hannah prayed to the Lord, weeping bitterly. And she made a vow, saying, "Lord Almighty, if you will only look on your servant's misery and remember me, and not forget your servant but give her a son, then I will give him to the Lord for all the days of his life, and no razor will ever be used on his head." As she kept on praying to the Lord, Eli observed her mouth. Hannah was praying in her heart, and her lips were moving but her voice was not heard. Eli thought she was drunk and said to her, "How long are you going to stay drunk? Put away your wine." "Not so, my lord," Hannah replied, "I am a woman

who is deeply troubled. I have not been drink-
ing wine or beer; I was pouring out my soul
to the Lord. Do not take your servant for a
wicked woman; I have been praying here out of
my great anguish and grief." Eli answered, "Go
in peace, and may the God of Israel grant you
what you have asked of him." She said, "May
your servant find favor in your eyes." Then she
went her way and ate something, and her face
was no longer downcast (1 Sam. 1:9–18, NIV).

The entire family got up early the next morning
and went to worship the LORD once more. Then
they returned home to Ramah. When Elkanah
slept with Hannah, the LORD remembered her
plea, and in due time she gave birth to a son.
She named him Samuel, for she said, "I asked
the LORD for him" (1 Sam. 1:19–20, NLT).

When Hannah gave God her steadfast love and
outstanding faith, God was not going to be outdone! He
stunned Hannah in return with the ultimate fruit: the
fruit of the womb. Hannah conceived a son from a previously barren womb. Although she had been through
what looked like many years of fruitless worship, this
woman would not give up! She did not allow her love for
God to be extinguished by her barrenness or Peninnah.

Hannah's move moved God's heart so powerfully that it instantly moved His hand on her behalf. Desperate people do desperate things!

Hannah's steadfast love and faith prompted God to respond to her ultimate trust in Him with the ultimate blessing, the gift of life. This miraculous turnaround was caused by Hannah's unshakeable faith. The Lord responded to a desperate woman's trust in Him by answering her impassioned, heartfelt plea. And Hannah's extravagant offering of a yet-to-be conceived child triggered a mighty move by God. Throughout her entire ordeal, Hannah was resolute in her commitment to God, never giving up on her expectation of a blessing from Him. She also kept her word after God's promise was fulfilled and brought the child back to the temple to serve God all the days of his life after he was weaned. Hannah gave her son the name Samuel, which means "asked of God," and the unbreakable bond between God and Hannah birthed a spectacular miracle.

Hannah's son Samuel grew up to became a mighty prophet of God with two books in the Bible named after him. Extraordinary faith produces extraordinary blessings.

Again, how should true lovers of God respond when they receive mind-blowing blessings from Him? Just like King David, Hannah filled the air with joyful words as she thanked God for His great kindness toward her. Hannah's prayer of dedication when she gave up her only child to the Lord revealed her gratitude to the one whom she had served so faithfully for so many years with tears. These words capture some of her enormous happiness:

> When the child was weaned, Hannah took him to the Tabernacle in Shiloh. They brought along a three-year-old bull for the sacrifice and a basket of flour and some wine (1 Sam. 1:24, NLT).

> Then Hannah prayed: "My heart rejoices in the Lord! The Lord has made me strong. Now I have an answer for my enemies; I rejoice because you rescued me. No one is holy like the Lord! There is no one besides you; there is no Rock like our God. Stop acting so proud and haughty! Don't speak with such arrogance! For the Lord is a God who knows what you have done; He will judge your actions. The bow of the mighty is now broken, and those who stumbled are now strong. Those who were well fed are now starving, and those who were starving are now full. The childless woman now has seven children, and the woman with many children wastes away. The Lord gives both death and life; He brings some down to the grave but raises others up. The Lord makes some poor and others rich; He brings some down and lifts others up. He

lifts the poor from the dust and the needy from the garbage dump. He sets them among princes, placing them in seats of honor. For all the earth is the Lord's and he has set the world in order. He will protect his faithful ones, but the wicked will disappear in darkness. No one will succeed by strength alone. Those who fight against the Lord will be shattered. He thunders against them from heaven; the Lord judges throughout the earth, He gives power to his king; He increases the strength of his anointed one."

Then Elkanah returned home to Ramah without Samuel. And the boy served the Lord by assisting Eli the priest (1 Sam. 2; 1–11, NLT).

"But Samuel, though he was only a boy, served the Lord. He wore a linen garment like that of a priest (1 Sam. 2:18, NLT).

After the dedication of her son into His service, God again responded to Hannah with great magnanimity. He was not done giving her fruits and rewards for her ultimate devotion to Him. God would not send Hannah home empty-handed to receive fresh insults from Peninnah after her faithful trust in Him for still not having any children by her side. When they returned back home, God decided to do this for His devout daughter: "Indeed the Lord visited Hannah, and she conceived and bore three sons and two daughters. And the boy Samuel grew in the presence of the LORD" (1 Sam. 2:21, ESV).

God blessed Hannah with five more children! You really cannot outgive God. Take that on the chin, Peninnah!

> Those who sow with tears will reap with songs of joy (Ps. 126:5, NIV).

> So let's not get tired of doing what is good. At just the right time we will reap a harvest of blessing if we don't give up (Gal. 6:9, NIV).

All of Hannah's children were the direct fruit of her steadfast trust in God. The Lord comforted Hannah for her painful past, and we learn from her experience that no one can ever comfort or reward us as He can. We must expect great things from a great and awesome God. After enduring many years of tremendous adversity, Hannah won her battle with barrenness. God can be trusted, and we can be assured that there will be abundant fruits for our devotion to Him. Our final lesson from Hannah on giving God ultimate love is this:

> *Will we still love God, be persistent in prayer, and continue to give Him unstoppable worship when we are confronted with negative life circumstances? Or will we let negative circumstances extinguish our love for Him?*

18

Offerings of True Devotion: Elizabeth and Zechariah

N ow let's take a look at the valuable lessons to be gained from the lives of Elizabeth and her husband. They were from a family of priests and served God dutifully from their youth. Although this couple was also barren, they continued to live righteously before God, and carefully obeyed all His commandments. Even as the black hairs on their heads turned gray, they did not stop loving and serving Him. Due to their advanced age, they had lost all hope of ever conceiving their own children, but unlike Hannah, Elizabeth was the sole recipient of her husband's love; Elizabeth did not have a second wife to contend with. Their barrenness was still no less of a stigma and source of heartache for this devoted couple.

When Herod was king of Judea, there was a
Jewish priest named Zechariah. He was a
member of the priestly order of Abijah, and his
wife, Elizabeth, was also from the priestly line
of Aaron. Zechariah and Elizabeth were righteous in God's eyes, careful to obey all of the
Lord's commandments and regulations. They
had no children because Elizabeth was unable
to conceive, and they were both very old (Luke
1:5–7, NLT).

As they neared the end of their lives, the dream of
ever having children appeared to be completely over,
and if they had been bitter deep within their hearts after
loving and serving God for so long, it would be easy for
us all of to understand. We can also imagine the pain
they felt each time a newborn baby was dedicated at the
temple. We again see the picture of true lovers of God
living their lives honoring Him while their plight seems
to be completely ignored by God.

As was the case with Hannah, they did not change
their hearts toward God. They served Him faithfully day
and night, although He appeared to have completely
forgotten about them. He had not answered their many
pleas, but the two continued to serve Him while wrestling with their infertility. Many onlookers would have
privately or even publicly mocked them for what looked

like fruitless service to God, but Elizabeth and Zechariah continued to love God.

Many in their region would also have birthed and reared healthy children. Some of those babies themselves would have become adults with children of their own. But Elizabeth and Zechariah continued to lack one of life's greatest blessings. The couple, however, remained steadfast in their love for God. Neither of them allowed their love for Him or one another to grow cold. Instead they yielded their whole hearts and lives to God in worshipful submission. The first important lesson is that you have not been forgotten by God, even though it may seem that you have. If we are willing to give God our ultimate trust, unexpected miracles will happen in our own lives too.

God is more faithful than we are and never forgets His beloved and faithful children.

Elizabeth and Zechariah were definitely too old to consider having children of their own, but a spectacular miracle was about to unfold in their lives!

One day while Zechariah's division was on duty and he was serving as priest before God, he was chosen by lot, according to the custom of the priesthood, to enter the temple of the Lord and burn incense. And at the hour of the incense offering, the entire congregation was praying outside. Just then, an angel of the Lord appeared to Zechariah, standing at the right side of the altar of the incense. When Zechariah saw him, he was startled and overcome with fear. But the angel said to him, "Do not be afraid, Zechariah, because your prayer has been heard. Your wife Elizabeth will bear you a son, and you shall give him the name John. He will be a joy and delight to you, and many will rejoice at his birth, for he will be great in the sight of the Lord. He shall never take wine or strong drink, and he will be filled with the Holy Spirit even from his mother's womb. Many of the sons of Israel he will turn back to the Lord their God. And he will go on before the Lord in the spirit and power of Elijah, to turn the hearts of the fathers to their children, and the disobedient to the wisdom of the righteous— to make ready a people prepared for the Lord." "How can I be sure of this?" Zechariah asked the angel. "I am an old man, and my wife is well along in years." "I am Gabriel," replied the angel. "I stand in the presence of God, and I have been sent to speak to you and to bring you this good news. And now you will be silent and unable to speak until the day this comes to pass, because you did not believe my words, which will be fulfilled at their proper time."...When the time came for Elizabeth to have her child, she gave birth to a son. Her neighbors and relatives heard that the Lord had shown her great mercy, and they rejoiced with her" (Luke 1:8–17, 18–20, 57–58, BSB).

Zechariah was so shocked by the awesome good news that even during a supernatural encounter with an angel, his doubt persisted. Reality had gotten the better of him, and he immediately blurted out the obvious to the awesome angelic messenger. "How can I be sure of this?" Zechariah asked the angel. God in His loving kindness understood Zechariah's incredulity at the amazing turn of events, and although He chastised him for not believing the angel's words, God finally blessed the couple with their own child after so many years of barrenness. Elizabeth gave birth to their son, John. Elizabeth and Zechariah receive special mention in the Bible for their devotion to God. Their son, John, would be no ordinary child, either. He would gain great fame and prominence as the forerunner to the Lord Jesus Christ.

God is not unjust; he will not forget your work and the love you have shown him as you have helped his people and continue to help them (Heb. 6:10, NIV).

Can a mother forget the baby at her breast and
have no compassion on the child she has borne?
Though she may forget, I will not forget you!
(Isa. 49:15, NIV).

The lives of Hannah and Elizabeth remind us of
other great women in the Bible who struggled with barrenness. They all received extraordinary children after
their intense wrestling with barrenness. Sarah, Rebekah,
and Samson's mother all received miraculous children
from God after experiencing lengthy periods of barrenness, and their testimonies continue to bless many generations of people. All the children produced from these
intense struggles accomplished great things for God, and
their testimonies have continued to encourage us. For
true lovers of God, "nothing is impossible with God!"
(Luke 1:37, NLT).

Ultimate trust in God yields ultimate blessings from
Him.

Praise the Lord. Praise the Lord, you his servants; praise the name of the Lord. Let the
name of the Lord be praised, both now and
forevermore. From the rising of the sun to the
place where it sets, the name of the Lord is to be
praised. The Lord is exalted over all the nations,
his glory above the heavens. Who is like the
Lord our God the One who sits enthroned on

high, who stoops down to look on the heavens and the earth? He raises the poor from the dust and lifts the needy from the ash heap; He seats them with princes, with the princes of his people. He settles the childless woman in her home as a happy mother of children. Praise the Lord (Ps. 113, NIV).

How will you respond to God when it seems like your love and service toward Him are in vain?

19

Extravagant Love Produces Extravagant Worship

A $20,000 Jar of Perfume and the Magi

We are allowed to observe another great example of extravagant love for God by a woman the Bible refers to as a very sinful woman. She came to express her repentance to God by pouring out some very expensive perfume on Jesus. The jar of fragrance we're talking about here was not at all the cheap stuff. It was worth almost a year's wages! Translated into today's minimum wage, that would be at least $20,000. Most of us—myself included—will probably never own a fragrance this expensive, let alone pour it on a complete stranger. Onlookers would probably have considered her actions the onset of insanity. During those times, and possibly even nowadays, this would also be viewed as very inappropriate behavior from a woman toward a man, especially a holy man. The harsh rebukes, embarrassment, or any other price she would have to pay for her extravagant worship did not, however, deter this woman from displaying her love to God. What might have looked like irresponsible, wasteful spending to others was simply a genuinely repentant woman giving her extravagant worship to the Lord.

Uninvited, she had entered the home where Jesus was dining with the religious leaders of the day, and she went directly to Him. She began to pour the extremely expensive perfume on His head, not allowing the fear of being ridiculed for her outlandish offering to stop her. The woman then proceeded to do the menial task of washing Jesus' very dusty feet with her tears, a job many would be unwilling to do back then and something his host had not done. She finished by wiping the tears off His feet with her own hair. All the while she kissed and anointed Jesus' feet with the expensive perfume and wept profusely in genuine repentance. (See Mark 14:3–9.)

Her offering was a most extraordinary display of love toward God.

As expected her actions brought swift and severe criticism from the religious leaders and others who were present. "If this man were a prophet, he would know who is touching him and what kind of woman she is—that she is a sinner." "It could have been spent on the poor."

They murmured about both her sinful lifestyle and the value of the expensive perfume she had poured on Jesus. Just like King David before her, this woman's extravagant display of love toward God looked scandalous to others. But the woman was genuinely repenting for her sins and loving God. When you also consider the very low status women held in those days, her behavior must have looked very alarming to all.

Although her behavior was not considered proper in society, her love for God was plain for all to see, but to the religious leaders of the day there might not have been a more scandalous event during Jesus' public ministry. Even though people disapproved of her actions, the woman's worship of God was memorialized in the scriptures. Apparently this rare display of extravagant love, along with her sorrowful repentance, was completely accepted by Jesus.

She was not rejected by God because her offering was from a contrite heart, and this was very pleasing to Him. The onlookers, however, were wrong in their observations. Yes, it is indeed our Christian duty to give generously to the poor, and this, unfortunately, is needed more and more in our world, but we must also remember that God comes first. Without Him, we have no life, service, or gifts to give to anyone unless we first receive them from Him. Loving acts of generosity are a vital part of our Christian responsibility, and they are a clear mandate from God. We must, however, be extremely cautious about criticizing anyone's extravagant worship of God.

Lest we trigger unpleasant consequences in our own lives, as David's wife Princess Michal had, we must not judge another person's way of expressing love for God. Spending our lives and resources on God may not make us popular with people. It is, however, most pleasing to Him. Her extremely lavish worship and Jesus' response to it also clearly demonstrated the link between love and worship. Although she had led a very sinful life, her genuine repentance and extravagant love of God led to a complete pardon from Him. Her many wrongdoings were completely forgiven, and this woman instantly became a part of God's family. All sinners are welcomed by Jesus when they acknowledge and genuinely repent of their sins. Even the most egregious sins will be forgiven when we turn toward God in genuine repentance.

When the Pharisee who had invited him saw this, he said to himself, "If this man were a prophet, he would know who is touching him and what kind of woman she is—that she is a sinner."

Jesus answered him, "Simon, I have something to tell you."

"Tell me, teacher," he said.

"Two people owed money to a certain moneylender. One owed him five hundred denarii, and the other fifty. Neither of them had the money to pay him back, so he forgave the debts of both. Now which of them will love him more?"

Simon replied, "I suppose the one who had the bigger debt forgiven."

"You have judged correctly," Jesus said.

Then he turned toward the woman and said to Simon, "Do you see this woman? I came into your house. You did not give me any water for my feet, but she wet my feet with her tears and wiped them with her hair. You did not give me a kiss, but this woman, from the time I entered, has not stopped kissing my feet. You did not put oil on my head, but she has poured perfume on my feet. Therefore, I tell you, her many sins have been forgiven—as her great love has shown. But whoever has been forgiven little loves little."

Then Jesus said to her, "Your sins are forgiven" (Luke 7:39–48, NIV).

She is a reminder of the wonderful blessings that will follow when we choose to boldly express our love to God. Her outlandish worship was her way of giving God over-the-top, mega love. Recipients of God's ultimate grace ought to respond to God with extravagant love, according to the following words spoken by Jesus:

"So she has shown me much love. But a person who is forgiven little shows only little love" (Luke 7:47, NLT).

Love is at the root of worship and little love for God results in little worship to Him.

The woman poured out her expensive perfume on the Lord to demonstrate her love. Her actions serve as an example for all who desire to give God ultimate love. The greater our revelation of God's love and forgiveness is, the greater our expression of love toward Him will be.

Are we willing to offer God our extravagant love and sincere worship as this woman did? If so, what are we prepared to willingly present to our wonderful and glorious God?

The Magi

Another example of honoring God with generous gifts in the scriptures is the wise men, or Magi, who traveled from the East to worship the newborn child Jesus. These high-ranking, high-caliber men came from a very prosperous part of the world, yet they left their families, livelihoods, and other comforts to follow God. According to the account, they journeyed for months, guided only by a special star provided as a sign from God. These men trusted God completely and followed the heavenly body through all manner of weather. After overcoming many perils on their journey, they finally arrived where the child was, and they greatly rejoiced.

After Jesus was born in Bethlehem in Judea, during the time of King Herod, Magi from the east came to Jerusalem and asked, "Where is the one who has been born king of the Jews? We saw his star when it rose and have come to worship him."...On coming to the house, they saw the child with his mother Mary, and they bowed down and worshiped him. Then they opened their treasures and presented him with gifts of gold, frankincense and myrrh (Matt. 2:1–2, 11 NIV).

The sentiment of these devout men cannot be denied. It was clearly seen as they celebrated and thanked God for sending the Savior to the world. Their humble posture when they saw the little child was evidence of the reverence for God in their hearts. These impressive men, who deserved an audience with King Herod, all fell down to the ground, stretched out flat, and prostrated themselves to worship Jesus. The lavish gifts they also brought out from their treasures to give to Him revealed the extravagant love for God in their hearts. We are again reminded by all these people that giving God ultimate love or worship will cost us something and require willingness and dedication on our part.

It is not the value or size of our gifts that matters to God, but the love in our hearts toward Him.

We must always be careful not to analyze, wrongly interpret, or make disapproving remarks about other people's chosen expressions of worshipping God. We must all give according to the measure of our faith and in proportion to our abilities. That the monetary value of our gifts is not an issue with God was made abundantly clear in the example of the poor widow.

Her simple two copper coins were personally acknowledged by Jesus, and they were all that she had. Giving to God first from the very best of every blessing that comes to us is one way we can show our love to Him. The choice of whether to give God the leftovers or the most valuable part of our lives is always ours. It is not love if we feel compelled to offer it, and we must never give out of compulsion. "Each of you should give what you have decided in your heart to give, not reluctantly or under compulsion, for God loves a cheerful giver" (2 Cor. 9:7, NIV).

God is our treasure beyond price. Relegating our Creator to the very bottom of things is not the right attitude for a true worshipper. Joyfully loving God as David, Solomon, the Magi, Mary, and many others did is entirely up to our own free will. The recipient of our love is worthy. In a world that wants to shame us into not valuing God, we must be unapologetic about giving Him our best in every way we can.

Many believers in God exemplified true love for Him. They followed and obeyed Him, testifying of His great love wherever and in whatever way they had the opportunity. Whether in times of joy, temptation, trouble, or pain, they all yielded to God and faithfully served Him. This depth of love expressed as extreme submission to God produces great fruit in our lives. We have been challenged by all these exemplary models as they relinquished their all to God.

Are you willing to go long distances and do whatever God commands as a way of giving Him your mega love?

CHAPTER

20

In His Presence
I Daily Live

As we come toward the end of seeking answers in
our quest to give God ultimate love, some examples of devoted worship from early followers of Jesus
Christ will serve also as additional models for us. These
believers regularly came together to minister to God
before engaging in their various ministry activities, and
although they had many new responsibilities, they did
not allow their time alone with God to be hindered.

In the church at Antioch there were proph-
ets and teachers: Barnabas, Simeon called
Niger, Lucius of Cyrene, Manaen (a child-
hood companion of Herod the Tetrarch), and
Saul. While they were worshipping the Lord
and fasting, the Holy Spirit said, "Set apart for
Me Barnabas and Saul for the work to which

I have called them." So after they had fasted
and prayed, they laid their hands on them and
sent them off . . . . "For this is what the Lord
has commanded us: 'I have made you a light for
the Gentiles, to bring salvation to the ends of
the earth.'" When the Gentiles heard this, they
rejoiced and glorified the word of the Lord, and
all who were appointed for eternal life believed.
And the word of the Lord spread throughout
that region (Acts 13:1–3, 48–49, BSB).

They sought God regarding their own lives and the
lives of the new disciples who had come to the Lord. The
work He had entrusted to them was a labor of love, and
they stayed close to God through fasting, prayers, and
worship. These leaders did not let the pressure of work
push their time with God to last place, but they gathered
to minister to God before undertaking their numerous
assignments. The early Christians had discovered another
great principle we must all emulate: Love is at the core of
worship and worship precedes service. We must soak in
God's presence to be effective witnesses for Him.

Training new converts, meeting various needs,
urgent calls to go to diverse mission fields and many other
obligations swirled around them, but the early believers
prioritized their time with God. They honored Him with
unity of heart, mind, and purpose, and these early disciples understood that in God's presence was where all

the grace for effective Christ-like service lay. Prioritizing time alone with God and putting Him first in our daily lives will release all the power we need. It has also been said, "We must talk to God about people before talking to people about God." The Lord of the work comes before the work of the Lord. We must remind leaders not to get so caught up in the work of the Lord that they neglect spending time with the Lord of the work.

This is an important lesson on our journey, because for genuine fruitful Christian service, we must first seek the one who gave us that work or ministry. The disciples highly esteemed God and were careful not to treat the trust He had placed in them lightly. So great was their reverence for Him that they considered it an absolute necessity to hear from Him before going out to perform their duties. We also need to learn to wait on or minister to God before serving people. True worshippers correctly distinguish between their times for ministering to and serving people and their topmost priority of ministering to God. God-given assignments flourish only when we take full advantage of our access to God. Abiding in God's presence enables us to hear from His Holy Spirit and live rightly balanced lives. God will give us grace for every area of our lives when we seek Him, and our times with Him chase away all our doubts, fears, and insecurities. Our heavenly Father calms our troubled emotions as God's Holy Spirit refreshes us and gives us solutions to our challenges.

When we spend quality time with God, we receive clear direction from Him. He shows us where to go and with whom to go.

As we abide in Him daily, the truth from His word will be planted deep within our hearts and guide, correct, and lead us to beneficial life choices. True worshippers seek the Lord with all their hearts and stay in His presence until they hear His voice. Our hearts also become more open to His word, and this produces innumerable blessings in our lives. We read in the scriptures that one of the fruits of waiting in God's presence is that He makes known to us the right paths in life to follow.

You make known to me the path of life; in your presence there is fullness of joy; at your right hand are pleasures forevermore (Ps. 16:11, ESV).

Whether you turn to the right or to the left, your ears will hear a voice behind you, saying, "This is the way; walk in it" (Isa. 30:21, NIV).

This is what the LORD says—your Redeemer, the Holy One of Israel: "I am the LORD your God, who teaches you what is best for you, who directs you in the way you should go" (Isa. 48:17, NIV).

Again, we read about King David, a man who knew the value of spending quality time with God. He appointed full-time worshippers to honor and invoke God's presence, which brought tremendous blessings to his family and the entire nation: "David appointed the following Levites to lead the people in worship before the Ark of the LORD—to invoke his blessings, to give thanks, and to praise the LORD, the God of Israel" (1 Chron. 16:4, NLT).

As mentioned earlier, Samuel, the great judge and prophet of Israel, also began his ministry by first learning how to minister to God. "Now Samuel was ministering before the LORD, as a boy wearing a linen ephod" (1 Sam. 2:18, NASB). He lived in the temple and slept beside the ark that carried God's presence. After being dedicated into God's service at a tender age by his mother, Samuel spent his whole life faithfully serving God and grew to become a mighty servant of God.

Eli, the priest in charge of the ark before Samuel, did not revere or honor the Lord, nor did he value time in God's presence. God was very displeased with Eli's family because their wicked actions greatly tarnished their priestly calling. Although they continued to serve as priests in God's temple, they committed many outrageous atrocities and recklessly dishonored God. Eli's two sons, Hophni and Phinehas, had become scoundrels, and the two greatly profaned the Lord's name. They repeatedly violated His commands, and mocked Him among His people.

> Now the sons of Eli were scoundrels who had no respect for the LORD or for their duties as priests. Whenever anyone offered a sacrifice, Eli's sons would send over a servant with a three-pronged fork. While the meat of the sacrificed animal was still boiling, the servant would stick the fork into the pot and demand that whatever it brought up be given to Eli's sons. All the Israelites who came to worship at Shiloh were treated this way . . . . .Now Eli was very old, but he was aware of what his sons were doing to the people of Israel. He knew, for instance, that his sons were seducing the young women who assisted at the entrance of the Tabernacle (1 Sam. 2:12–14, 22, NLT).

Eli honored his children above God and refused to expel them from service. Although the ark that symbolized God's presence was in their midst, the family did not esteem or have any regard for God, and their hearts grew colder against Him with every wicked act. They continued to defy God more and more, and the entire family eventually received just punishment for their lack of repentance. Their actions brought great devastation upon their family and resulted in a stinging rebuke from the Lord.

Then a man of God came to Eli and said to him, "Thus says the LORD, 'Did I not indeed reveal Myself to the house of your father when they were in Egypt in bondage to Pharaoh's house? Did I not choose them from all the tribes of Israel to be My priests, to go up to My altar, to burn incense, to carry an ephod before Me; and did I not give to the house of your father all the fire offerings of the sons of Israel? Why do you kick at My sacrifice and at My offering which I have commanded in My dwelling, and honor your sons above Me, by making your-selves fat with the choicest of every offering of My people Israel?" (1 Sam. 2:27–29, NASB).

Therefore the LORD, the God of Israel, declares: "I promised that members of your family would minister before me forever." But now the LORD declares: "Far be it from me! Those who honor me I will honor, but those who despise me will be disdained. The time is coming when I will put an end to your family, so it will no longer serve as my priests. All the members of your family will die before their time. None will reach old age. You will watch with envy as I pour out prosperity on the people of Israel. But no members of your family will ever live out their days. Those who survive will live in sadness and grief, and their children will die a violent death. And to prove that what I have said will come true, I will cause your two sons, Hophni and Phinehas, to die on the same day! Then I will raise up a faithful priest who will serve me and do what I desire. I will establish his family, and they will be priests to my anointed kings forever" (1 Sam. 2:30–35, NIV).

Eli and his family are sad reminders of what can happen when God's servants no longer love or prioritize Him. As His representatives to the people, the primary responsibility of Eli's family was to set a good example of holiness to the people. The nation looked up to them as their leaders, and God had entrusted them with a sacred duty.

It is of utmost importance that we carefully foster, nourish, and guard our closeness to God. He is our source and sustainer.

Eli's successor, Samuel, was wise enough to learn from this family's errors and did not repeat their many mistakes. Before going about his daily duties, Samuel ministered to the Lord in front of the ark, spending quality time in God's presence. He was faithfully devoted to

God and did not neglect the great truth that worship precedes service. When our minds are not renewed by God daily, we can easily become overtaken by sin, as was the case with Eli and his sons. Neglecting the commandment to love the Lord your God with all our hearts, minds, and strength will reduce our service to Him to something done for appearances only. Dead works are null and void with God, so we need to renew this vital aspect of our relationship with Him.

We must not miss this most powerful weapon in our arsenal: God's presence. Victory in spiritual warfare and fruitful Christian service require that we make the necessary changes in our thinking and practices to put God first in our lives. Worshipping God is a way to show mega love for Him, which gives us supernatural invigoration when we are connected to the true source of spiritual power.

> But they that wait upon the Lord shall renew their strength; they shall mount up with wings as eagles; they shall run, and not be weary; they shall walk, and not faint (Isa. 40:31, English Revised Version).

> My eyes shall be upon the faithful of the land that they may dwell with me; He who walks in a blameless way is the one who will minister to me (Ps. 101:6, NASB).

One more outstanding example of serving God is found in the book of Ezekiel, which describes a family led by a man named Zadok. They received very special commendation from God for their loyal service and were specially recognized by Him when He stated how very pleased with them He was. Their household was a clear contrast to Eli and his family.

"But the Levites who went far from Me when Israel went astray, who went astray from Me after their idols, shall bear the punishment for their iniquity. Yet they shall be ministers in My sanctuary, having oversight at the gates of the house and ministering in the house; they shall slaughter the burnt offering and the sacrifice for the people, and they shall stand before them to minister to them. Because they ministered to them before their idols and became a stumbling block of iniquity to the house of Israel, therefore I have sworn against them," declares the Lord GOD, "that they shall bear the punishment for their iniquity. And they shall not come near to Me to serve as a priest to Me, nor come near to any of My holy things, to the things that are most holy; but they will bear their shame and their abominations which they have committed. Yet I will appoint them to keep charge of the house, of all its service and of all that shall be done in it. But the Levitical priests, the sons of Zadok, who kept charge of My sanctuary when the sons of Israel went astray from Me, shall come near to Me to minister to Me; and they shall stand before Me to offer Me the fat and the blood," declares the Lord GOD. "They shall enter My sanctuary; they shall come near to My table to minister to Me and keep My charge" (Ezek. 44:12–17, NASB).

Zadok prioritized loving and serving God before people. He would only serve the people in a way that pleased and honored God. The family's loyalty resulted in their being the only ones with exclusive access to God's presence, while others were only allowed to take care of the location and articles used for worship and were not allowed anywhere near God Himself.

Zadok's family was the only one that received this great honor because of their great devotion to God. They were wholly pleasing to Him in all their ways, and God expressed His appreciation to them. Imagine being specially honored by God Himself. There are many ministers who would be content with serving the people and attending to buildings, locations, and rituals of worship. They may never go any deeper in their walks with God, and without God's grace we cannot successfully run our race. Serving God comes before serving people.

By honoring and esteeming God in our hearts we show Him mega love. Are you willing to make the necessary changes to practice this vital truth?

21

He Fills My
Every Longing

B eautiful acts of praise and worship may already be
a part of our normal worship experience as followers of the Lord Jesus Christ. The scriptures encourage
us to open our mouths, shout aloud, sing praises, and
offer exuberant worship to God. Thanksgiving flows into
praise, and praise into worship, as we minister to the
Lord with music, songs, the spoken word, uplifted hands,
fasting, and prayers—these are all ways that we convey
our love to Him.

> Shout to the Lord, all the earth; break out in
> praise and sing for joy! Sing your praise to the
> Lord with the harp, with the harp and melodi-
> ous song, with trumpets and the sound of the
> ram's horn. Make a joyful symphony before the
> Lord (Ps. 98:4–6, NLT).

Let all that I am praise the Lord. O Lord my
God, how great you are! You are robed with
honor and majesty (Ps. 104:1, NIV).

I will praise you every day; yes, I will praise you
forever (Ps. 145:2, NLT).

Spending quality time to give God our love through
worship means that we acknowledge His goodness and
show our appreciation for His grace in our lives. This
brings us closer to Him and connects our hearts with
His. Giving thanks and praises to Him is the prerequisite for entering into His presence: "Enter his gates with
thanksgiving; go into his courts with praise. Give thanks
to him and praise his name" (Ps. 100:4, NLT).

However, a lot of attention is given to celebration
these days, but not enough truth is embraced about our
heart-to-heart connection with God. After the verse in
Psalm 100, we are taught to focus on God's wonderful
attributes and His faithful love: "For the Lord is good.
His unfailing love continues forever, and his faithfulness
continues to each generation" (Ps. 100:5, NLT).

If we are to go deeper into our time with Him, we
need to esteem God for who He is (His identity), and
not just for what He does (His activity in our lives). This
will take us deeper into our worship experience, and
the times we spend with God will culminate in greater
intimacy with Him. We don't want to spend our lives

at His gates and never fully experience His person and great house. A pastor at my local church observed that remaining at the gates or courts of a house would be like arriving in a country and spending the entire time on the airport tarmac. We cannot claim to have experienced a place, culture, or people if we have only experienced the arrival terminal at the airport. We must go deeper to experience the place, people, and culture. If we choose to stay at the gates or courts of God's great house, the greatest danger will be always being too close to the exit! The innermost sanctuary of our hearts is the place where we share deepest intimacy with God, and when we offer God our hearts, our lives will be transformed. Our labor for Him will also flow from a place of love as we recall all that God has done for us. This is giving Him mega love.

Let all that I am praise the LORD; with my whole heart, I will praise his holy name. Let all that I am praise the LORD; may I never forget the good things he does for me (Ps. 103:1–2, NLT).

The LORD is my strength and my defense; he has become my salvation. He is my God, and I will praise him, my father's God, and I will exalt him (Exod. 15:2, NIV).

With praise and thanksgiving they sang to the LORD: "He is good; his love toward Israel endures forever." And all the people gave a great shout of praise to the LORD, because the foundation of the house of the LORD was laid (Ezra 3:11, NIV).

God expresses the desire to have a fiercely passionate relationship with us. He is not interested in a tepid union at all. He spoke these words to one of the seven churches in the book of Revelation: "I know your deeds; you are neither cold nor hot. How I wish you were one or the other. So because you are lukewarm—neither hot nor cold—I am about to spit you out of My mouth!" (Rev. 3:15–16, BSB).

When we've known a person for a long time, we may start to take him for granted. Being a Christian for what seems like a long time can make us forget to be in awe of God. Much of our enthusiasm for Him may have waned, and we may lose focus on who He is and why we worship Him. Although it may be unintentional, showing any disregard for God is dangerous. To fulfill our destinies as true worshippers, we must eagerly pursue Him. He has already demonstrated His passion for us; all that remains is a response on our part. Lying deep within the heart of every true worshipper is a longing for more of God. There is no middle ground when it comes to loving God, and a genuine worshipper delights in the prospect of a closer union with God. Our yearning for Him should never be dismissed, because we are created to be loved by God, and our love for Him is not always easy to express with words. When we daily abide in His presence, He strengthens, refreshes, and replenishes every area of our lives.

Every heart that loves God needs to let Him know it. We must be hot, not cold or lukewarm. God wants all of us or none at all.

Having a passion for God will involve our emotions, and God wants our hearts' longings to lead us to Him. Many Christians are taught to repress their emotions. This may not always be the right response and is not emotionally healthy. We may have the mindset that strong or passionate feelings must always be controlled or contained. This is wisdom when it comes to our negative emotions, but not when it comes to loving God. God wants His children to express their feelings toward Him passionately through worship.

Our emotions are a gift from God and are given as prompts or cues when something needs our focus or attention. We may not always be able to share our true feelings even with those closest to us, but God created us and knows us best. He can be trusted with our lives and feelings. Not all emotions are pretty; if given full vent, some of our feelings would scare or harm those around us. Anger, for example, can lead to violence, and if not completely surrendered to God, anger can make us say and do things we may later regret. However, God is not intimidated by the extremes we may go through, and He can handle all of our emotions all of the time. God accepts us just as we are, and we were created in the image and likeness of a loving God. Our Creator expresses a wide range of emotions. They can range from love, joy, delight, and sorrow, to anger, fury, or even wrath at evil or injustice. God handles all His emotions in a healthy manner and wants us to do the same.

The LORD delights in those who fear him, who put their hope in his unfailing love (Ps. 147:11, NIV).

Jesus wept (John 11:35, NIV).

Then Jesus went into the temple courts and drove out all who were buying and selling there. He overturned the tables of the money changers and the seats of those selling doves. And He declared to them, "It is written: 'My house will be called a house of prayer.' But you are making it 'a den of robbers'" (Matt. 21:12–13, BSB).

And he passed in front of Moses, proclaiming, "The LORD, the LORD, the compassionate and gracious God, slow to anger, abounding in love and faithfulness" (Exod. 34:6, NIV).

But the LORD is the true God; he is the living God, the eternal King. When he is angry, the earth trembles; the nations cannot endure his wrath (Jer. 10:10, NIV).

Our feelings toward others should be expressed only within safe and healthy boundaries. Whether we are rejoicing, angry, sad, or grieving, our emotions are never to be disregarded or stifled. Instead, we are to bring them into our intimate times with God in worship. In God's presence, we can safely express our hearts and worship God individually or corporately. He fills our hearts with His joy, and this brings healing, restoration, strength, and deliverance to all aspects of our lives. Regardless of our circumstances, God's presence is the safest and healthiest place to let our emotions out. Whether our feelings are about God, other people, or our circumstances, we maintain healthy emotional balance when we place our emotions under the control of the Holy Spirit. This is also a way to honor God. By not saying and doing things to dishonor Him, we are giving Him our love. Reach out today for God's help and ask Him to help you get it together and hold it together. Spending quality time in God's presence will heal and satisfy our every longing.

Don't be dejected and sad, for the joy of the LORD is your strength! (Neh. 8:10, NLT).

Always be full of joy in the Lord. I say it again—
rejoice! (Phil. 4:4, NLT).

You will seek me and find me when you seek
me with all your heart (Jer. 29:13, NIV).

The life of Jesus gives us a perfect model of bringing
offerings of true love to God even when we are in deep
distress.

Relationships face their greatest challenges not
during the good times but in times of great difficulty.
When love is stretched and tested, it will grow much
stronger if it endures. Our union with God may also
sometimes be challenged by adversity, but during those
moments, if we remain steadfast in our love for Him, in
spite of the forces of darkness and life's greatest difficulties, we will be giving Him our mega love. These are all
parts of what it truly means to give God ultimate love.

Loving and seeking God prepares us for what God
has prepared for us. May God grant each one of us the
grace to love, trust, and obey Him at all times. It cannot
be overstated that God is the only one who deserves our
ultimate love, and yielding to Him when our will crosses
with His is one of the ways we can give Him mega love.
When we have doubts about God's existence, justice,
or fairness, we must obtain answers directly from Him
through His word, the Bible. Even when our emotions
are intensely negative, they must not be shut down. They

are to be safely addressed in God's presence as the deep within us crying out to the deep in God. One of the twelve psalms attributed to the sons of Korah gives us a glimpse of yearning for God in the following verses.

As the deer pants for streams of water, so my soul pants for you, my God (Ps. 42:1, NIV).

Deep waters call out to what is deeper still; at the roar of your waterfalls all your breakers and your waves swirled over me (Ps. 42:7, International Standard Version).

Heartfelt longings are urges for more of God. It is not wise to stifle our feelings; instead, we must let them bring us closer to God. We will find relief and fulfilment in Him. God gives His children access to all He is and has and owns everything. He holds nothing back from us, and all of heaven's vast resources are available to each one of us. We can eat freely at God's table at no charge.

Come, all you who are thirsty, come to the waters; and you who have no money, come, buy and eat! Come, buy wine and milk without money and without cost. Why spend money on what is not bread, and your labor on what does not satisfy? Listen, listen to me, and eat what is good, and you will delight in the richest of fare.

Give ear and come to me; listen, that you may live . . . . Seek the Lord while he may be found; call on him while he is near. Let the wicked forsake their ways and the unrighteous their thoughts. Let them turn to the Lord, and he will have mercy on them, and to our God, for he will freely pardon . . . . You will go out in joy and be led forth in peace; the mountains and hills will burst into song before you, and all the trees of the field will clap their hands (Isa. 55; 1–3, 6–7, 12, NIV).

Worship is initiated by longing for more of God, and God's presence satisfies our every longing.

Have you decided that God is worthy to receive your ultimate love? How you will demonstrate your own mega, over-the-top love for Him?

22

True and
False Lovers

rue and false lovers may use the words "I love you,"
but only one of these types of people truly means
these words. This is why our talk is also not proof enough
of genuine love for God. The way to distinguish a true
lover from a false one is by their fruits or walk and not
just by their talk. "You can identify them by their fruit,
that is, by the way they act. Can you pick grapes from
thornbushes, or figs from thistles?" (Matt. 7:16, NLT).
The way people begin to relate to and treat us is the real
evidence of their professed love.

If they talk love but act hate, neglect, or abuse, then
we know their words are not true, and we may need to
separate ourselves from such falsehoods. While a false
lover uses the words "I love you" to deceive, seduce, and
take advantage of another, a true lover genuinely means
those words and acts in accordance with them.

We are also told in the scriptures that God differentiates between true and false lovers or worshippers. When we gather together to worship, He is looking for those who will love and worship Him in spirit and in truth from a sincere heart and an obedient lifestyle.

> Jesus replied, "Believe me, dear woman, the time is coming when it will no longer matter whether you worship the Father on this mountain or in Jerusalem. You Samaritans know very little about the one you worship, while we Jews know all about him, for salvation comes through the Jews. But the time is coming—indeed it's here now—when true worshipers will worship the Father in spirit and in truth. The Father is looking for those who will worship him that way. For God is Spirit, so those who worship him must worship in spirit and in truth" (John 4:21–24, NLT).

The use of the adjective *true* to distinguish between worshippers means that, from God's vantage point, not everyone who shows up and professes to worship Him is a true lover of God. A quick look at the definition of the word *true* helps us to further understand the observation being made. *True* means "authentic, strictly genuine, real, not faked."

False, on the other hand, means "appearing to be the thing denoted but not so, deliberately made or meant to deceive, untrue, counterfeit, and fraudulent."

Jesus would not have made this distinction between worshippers if all worshippers of God were true. If there are true ones, then there must be false ones, as His words indicate.

God is seeking for true worshippers to worship Him. A genuine lover of God obeys His word and is empowered by His Holy Spirit. This is true worship. Obedience to God and true worship of Him originates from submitted hearts. True worshippers are always identifiable by their union with God, not by their church affiliations or labels (Baptists, Methodists, Pentecostals, or charismatics). These verses relate to the condition of our hearts, and God has made salvation through Jesus Christ the only prerequisite for a restored relationship with Him. The size of the crowd or magnificence of the location of worship has no bearing on true worship. Those who have repented of their sins and received God's free pardon through the payment made for our sins by Jesus Christ are the only ones He recognizes as true worshippers.

People who are not in a right relationship with God may fill our pews, but God will not recognize them as true worshippers. God is looking for people who will genuinely love Him from their hearts.

Authentic lovers of God have genuine Christlikeness. After we place our trust in Jesus Christ as Savior and Lord, following after God's ways must be the ongoing pursuit of a true lover of God or genuine worshipper. The way we choose to live our lives reveals whose children we really are, whether we are genuine sons and daughters of God or offspring of the fallen, satanic god of this world.

God reveals His nature through us. The scriptures we just read say that the Father is seeking those who will live in agreement with His word and be empowered by His Holy Spirit, in spirit and truth. If we seek to worship God in spirit and truth, then our new identities as sons and daughters of God must be affirmed by our walk and not just by our talk.

But to all who believed him and accepted him, he gave the right to become children of God (John 1:12, NLT).

For his Spirit joins with our spirit to affirm that we are God's children (Rom. 8:16, NIV).

For those who are led by the Spirit of God are the children of God (Rom. 8:14, NIV).

In contrast to true worshippers, there will be false ones. False worshippers get caught up in the trappings of religious affiliations, titles, status, rituals, locations, buildings, and other things instead of a genuine relationship with God. They substitute religious activities in place of wholehearted love for God but do not yield themselves to God's word; instead, they only appear to do so.

They may also participate in endless activities and meaningless programs that emanate from man-made ideas but not from God. These falsehoods will not produce victory in their lives or enable false worshippers to enter into a true union with God. They only cover themselves with religious fig leaves, just as Adam and Eve attempted to do after they failed to obey God. Worship in spirit and truth is not made evident by the number of religious activities we participate in or the pedigree of the churches we attend.

True worship flows from lives that are rooted in the truth of God's word and led continuously by His Holy Spirit. Instead of the true righteousness that comes only from God, false worshippers will cover themselves with self-righteousness, but God cannot be hoodwinked! We may be able to fool people for a while, but we can never fool God. Our fake walk will eventually come through in the ways we live our lives. False worshippers must take full responsibility for their sins and turn back to God in genuine repentance. This will change their status from false to true. Our heavenly Father is reaching out to all who are lost, asking them, "Where are you?" We must stop hiding from Him.

Then the eyes of both of them were opened, and
they realized they were naked; so they sewed
fig leaves together and made coverings for
themselves. Then the man and his wife heard
the sound of the LORD God as he was walking
in the garden in the cool of the day, and they
hid from the LORD God among the trees of the
garden. But the LORD God called to the man,
"Where are you?" He answered, "I heard you
in the garden, and I was afraid because I was
naked; so I hid" (Gen. 3:7–10, NIV).

God promises to be in our midst when we gather
in His name and serve Him. His presence will be visible
in our lives when true worship takes place. False worshippers are unable to enter into the genuine spiritual
union that takes place when we yield our hearts to God.
Let us set the highest standards for loving God and
reject the falsehood of self-righteousness or fake piety
that can never replace the genuine righteousness that
comes from God.

Authentic worship happens only when those
who truly love God come together to honor Him and
strengthen their connection with Him.

Obedient submission to God is the drumbeat of a
bona fide believer's heart. In all we think, say, and do,
we need to abide in God's truth so that our relationship
with Him can grow and deepen. When we stay in close

connection with the ones we love, we become closer to them and our relationship is strengthened. So by spending quality time in God's presence during Spirit-initiated and -infused worship, we also reinforce our relationship with Him.

Worship in spirit and in truth is the hallmark of a true lover of God. Let's ask ourselves the following questions regarding our own walks with God.

What is the current status of my own walk with God?

What are the attributes of a genuine lover or worshipper of God?

Do I love God with all of my heart, soul, strength, and assets?

Have other things and people taken priority over loving God in my life?

Can I reorganize, reprioritize, or release some of the things vying for my attention to put God first?

Finally, how do I stay alert so I don't reset my affection on other people and things instead of God?

Giving ourselves honest answers to these questions can be followed with praying these simple words:

Lord I thank you for your love for me. Please help me to yield to your grace in all my ways. I want to love you with my whole heart. Help me not to withhold any part of myself from you. Without you I can be, do, and have nothing. I receive your strength by faith through Jesus Christ my Savior. Amen.

But we must also remember that without His help, we can be and do nothing. Don't allow your answers to these questions to discourage or deter you from giving God all your love. Resist any temptation to allow guilt, fear, or any other sense of unworthiness to prevent you from trusting in God and continually turning to Him in genuine heartfelt conversations, which are called prayer. As you do this, He will fill your heart with love for Him. God delights in blessing us and bringing us back into His family and restoring His original plan for our lives.

To be effective witnesses of God's grace, we must first be true worshippers. Are you willing to make a fresh commitment to God?

23

More Than a Song

Do we really realize how pivotal faithfully loving God—worship—is to our existence? You might ask, how so? If worship was not so important, why was it one of the three major temptations Jesus had to go through at the beginning of His earthly ministry? Would Jesus love God enough to remain loyal to Him when faced with the pressure of temptation?

Loving God involves more than singing songs to Him. Whom we choose to follow and obey is foundational to worship and is the key to living successful lives. Satan used the issue of worshipping God as a powerful weapon in the lives of Jesus and Adam and Eve. He usurped God's authority and successfully overthrew the first two human beings when they chose to obey Satan rather than God. The second time around, he tried to thwart God's plan to rescue fallen human beings by craftily presenting Jesus with the choice of whom He would show His faithful allegiance to.

The devil said to him, "If you are the Son of God, tell this stone to become bread." Jesus answered, "It is written: 'Man shall not live on bread alone.'" The devil led him up to a high place and showed him in an instant all the kingdoms of the world. And he said to him, "I will give you all their authority and splendor; it has been given to me, and I can give it to anyone I want to. If you worship me, it will all be yours." Jesus answered, "It is written: 'Worship the Lord your God and serve him only'" (Luke 4:3–8, NIV).

Satan became the god of this world when Adam and Eve bowed to him, and he attempted to tempt Jesus to do the same. In Satan's new plot to destroy humankind and maintain his deceptive supremacy over our planet, the question of whom Jesus would obey or bow down to was a central theme. During His temptation in the wilderness, Jesus, the Savior of the world, had to choose whether to obey God or abuse His God-given powers to receive the enemy's promised protection, nourishment, personal wealth, fame, and glory.

Human beings disobeyed God in the garden of Eden, but Jesus would not repeat this grave error. God Himself came to the earth in human form to ensure the successful outcome of His plan to rescue human beings. To successfully complete His earthly ministry, Jesus had to answer this central question: Whom would He wholly devote Himself to? Satan's temptations would not have been enticing if they were not real. Jesus had to overcome all the temptations Satan presented to Him and chose not to exchange His allegiance to God for the enemy's promised advantages. He completely defeated the same ploy that had been used to destroy the first two human beings.

God is the true source of all blessings. He originally gave humankind dominion over all of the kingdoms of this world, and whom we decide to obey, follow, and worship determines the source of our global dominance, wealth, fame, and power. All that was being promised to Jesus by Satan was transferred to him when the first two human beings followed the enemy's words instead of God. They allowed themselves to be deceived. Adam and Eve lost their lives and everything they owned. Our planet was turned over to Satan, and he can now temporarily and falsely hand power, fame, and splendor over to whoever will worship or bow down to him.

At different points and in different ways in our own lives, the choice of serving a false god or letting God continue to be our source and sustainer will be presented to each one of us.

> But remember the LORD your God, for it is he who gives you the ability to produce wealth, and so confirms his covenant, which he swore to your ancestors, as it is today (Deut. 8:18, NIV).

The blessing of the LORD makes a person rich,
and he adds no sorrow with it (Prov. 10:22,
NLT).

Worshipping God means more than singing songs
to Him. Our belief in God and His ability to protect,
provide for, guide, and care for us are central to how
power and provision are released to human beings on the
earth. The decision on which kingdom to be a part of—
the dominion of God/light or the kingdom of Satan/
darkness—will be presented to every one of us. Whom
we obey and worship is the most crucial decision we will
make in our lifetimes. If we extravagantly love God in
worship, we will not be overtaken by the wicked plots of
the enemy. Our obedience to Him will be fueled by love
and not by our own will or works. The choice before all
of us is to believe in God or not. The presence of God is
the ultimate blessing produced in the life of a true lover
of God. A life lived trusting in and being obedient to
God is the only thing that will truly set us apart from
this world.

The LORD replied, "My Presence will go with
you, and I will give you rest." Then Moses said
to him, "If your Presence does not go with us,
do not send us up from here. How will anyone
know that you are pleased with me and with
your people unless you go with us? What else

will distinguish me and your people from all the other people on the face of the earth?" (Exod. 33:14–16, NIV).

Again, if loving God through worship is not crucial to our lives, why was it the theme of the epic "let my people go" battle that took place between Moses and Pharaoh in the land of Egypt? (Exod. 9:1). God wanted His people to be free to love, honor, and worship Him, so He demanded their release from Egypt. Giving His people freedom to worship Him was the main reason for the great struggle between the representative of God (personified by Moses) and the forces of darkness (personified by Pharaoh). The entire battle was about God's wanting His people to be His and not Pharaoh's. (See Exodus 5:1, 8:1, 8:20, and 9:13.)

Pharaoh was completely obliterated by God for resisting and opposing Him. Our Creator alone deserves all of our worship. Both Moses and Jesus depended solely on God's word as their only way out of temptation, and God's will, of course, always wins the day. His word is all we need to triumph over evil, and if it was good enough for Jesus, then it is good enough for us. Our hearts were created to love God and each other. Spending time with and enjoying God is the ultimate lovefest.

We also need to be about God's business in these end times. True success comes to us when we live a lifestyle that honors God. What is being passed off as worship today may not be authentic worship. A lifestyle of loving and honoring God has been replaced with a feel-good spirit for the sole purpose of drawing larger crowds to our churches. There may now be a generation of people who have never really experienced God's presence or His mighty power. Highly skilled musicians and artists have been hired to entertain and thrill Christian audiences, but worship in spirit and truth consists of more than singing great songs to God.

Many have not yet truly tasted the splendor and beauty of God's presence or had life-transforming encounters with him. Musical celebrations labeled worship have replaced genuine heart-to-heart worship. The role of true psalmists has been taken over by fame-seeking artists and musicians, and more than we may care to admit, skilled hirelings have displaced true worshippers in many of our churches. I am sad to be the one to suggest that we may have substituted the glory of what money can buy us for the real glory of God.

Things as they stand today may cause many churches to fail in their duties of being God's ambassadors on the earth. We are not impacting the souls we have been called to witness to, and lives are not being connected to the life-changing presence of God. False lifestyles are currently being passed off as true, and many people in our congregations do not really know or desire God. This will not offer real help or victory when people face life's difficulties, and just as a child is the public manifestation or blessing of a private act, the times we spend in God's presence will produce delightful blessings in our lives. The things we need and desire come as a direct result of spending time in His presence. Wonderful things happen when we initiate intimate times with God, and if we truly submit our lives to Him, the results in our ministries and churches will be far superior to anything we can do in our own strength.

There is no fruit without a root, and God's grace is awesome power. We receive His saving and enabling grace when we spend time with God.

Because we are falling short in the vital area of authentic worship, breathtaking stage productions and brilliant performances are now substitutes for the presence of God in our midst. We now bask in the glow of the newly favored blue stage light while attempting to imitate God's real presence. Energies generated by large crowds gathering together to sing and enjoy great moments together using the best and most advanced technologies and talents have turned God's house into an entertainment venue.

It is wonderful to upgrade and enhance our worship with the latest technologies, but we cannot use them to substitute for God's real presence.

Many have replaced real encounters with God with man-made facsimiles. People get so carried away by the excitement and euphoria during our gatherings that their lack of a true connection with God may be lost on them until they face life's storms. We must promptly cease from these mere appearances of genuine worship, because the consequences for many souls are truly frightening. People are slipping away into an eternity without God after attending these contrived services. They do not really know that they have not met with or truly experienced God, and this also leads to emptiness in their hearts. Have we become so desirous of this world that the priceless treasures that come from God no longer attract us? People are desperate and hungry for deliverance from their broken lives. To falsely convince them that they are experiencing God when they are not is an extremely grave matter. We must repent quickly of this and fervently seek God in a fresh way.

Genuine worship from submitted lives is what will really connect us to God's presence.

Salvation and freedom from all manner of bondage, healing, restoration, and every other blessing flow freely to us when we are really in God's presence. If we give God a fresh response to His already revealed word and genuinely reconnect our hearts to Him, our churches and gatherings will no longer trade a real connection with God for the trappings of false worldly success. We may be attracting larger crowds, but are people meeting with and encountering God in our midst?

It's not too late to confess and repent for not worshipping Him in spirit and in truth. The type of enduring faith and deep love for God that we see in the lives of the individuals we have learned from so far should be the norm in our Christian experience. Ordinary people like us can give God their mega love, and He in return gives us His. The supernatural results that ensue transform lives, and people are never the same as they were after encountering Him. It is also not enough to rely solely on miracles and supernatural happenings in our midst as evidence that God is present. These may be false measures.

> For false messiahs and false prophets will appear and perform great signs and wonders to deceive, if possible, even the elect. See, I have told you ahead of time (Matt. 24:24–25, NIV).

> The coming of the lawless one will be in accordance with how Satan works. He will use all sorts of displays of power through signs and wonders that serve the lie, and all the ways that wickedness deceives those who are perishing. They perish because they refused to love the truth and so be saved (2 Thess. 2:9–10, NIV).

A life lived in full obedience to and trust in God is what sets God's people apart.

Where necessary, we need to repent for lusting after things other than God and also take to heart a dire warning given to us regarding the last days we are living in. The proliferation of signs all around us makes many believe that these are such times. We are warned that wickedness will greatly increase on the earth and love for God will grow cold in many hearts. People will turn away from having faith in Him, and human beings will become more hateful, committing all manner of atrocities. I don't know about you, but the mere thought of my love for God ever going cold makes me shudder! We must by all means prevent this from happening; we must not only prevent it but also resolve in our hearts to love God in the highest way imaginable. We need to strengthen our union with Him.

> At that time many will turn away from the faith and will betray and hate each other, and many false prophets will appear and deceive many people. Because of the increase of wickedness, the love of most will grow cold (Matt 24:10–12, NIV).

> But understand this that in the last days there will come times of difficulty. For people will be lovers of self, lovers of money, proud, arrogant, abusive, disobedient to their parents, ungrateful, unholy, heartless, unappeasable, slanderous, without self-control, brutal, not loving good, treacherous, reckless, swollen with conceit, lovers of pleasure rather than lovers of God,

having the appearance of Godliness, but deny-
ing its power (2 Tim. 3:1–5, ESV).

We must not become casualties in the epidemic of
cold love toward God and people that will be prevalent in
our days. Instead we must fan into flames a love for God
in our hearts that will be impossible to extinguish. The
cooling of love for God and one another is a very dangerous thing and will lead to adverse outcomes. Overcoming the darkness that is growing daily in our world will
require nothing less than giving God His rightful first
place in our hearts. Great evil is now present in the earth,
and this calls for an authentic walk with God. This is an
invitation to us to return to our first love.

Let us come back in line with God's word, the
Bible, in our choices, practices, and lifestyles, and allow
everything in our lives to be in perfect harmony with
Him. His blessing on our lives makes us a blessing to
others. Devoting ourselves to God, as the early disciples
did, will give us the necessary strength to be effective
witnesses and leaders on God's behalf. Early followers
of Jesus Christ placed their complete trust in Him, and
time alone with God was prioritized above every other
endeavor. This resulted in wisdom, guidance, and instructions being received from the Holy Spirit that led to significant increase for God's kingdom. (See Acts 13:1–3,
48–49.) The prodigious productivity we observe in their
lives will also be our experience if we will practice the

principles they walked in. When we stay connected to the true vine, our lives are wonderfully transformed, and we become partners with God in the awesome task of restoring His lost family.

> Yes, I am the vine; you are the branches. Those who remain in me, and I in them, will produce much fruit. For apart from me you can do nothing (John 15:5, NLT).

> You did not choose me, but I chose you and appointed you so that you might go and bear fruit—fruit that will last—and so that whatever you ask in my name the Father will give you (John 15:16, NIV).

We have already learned about Samuel, who ministered to the Lord daily beside the ark and was enabled to hear God's call on his life although he was still quite young. Samuel ushered Israel into a new prophetic era because he spent quality time daily with God, and his leadership was revered by both the king and the entire nation. They all sought and submitted to his counsel. He offered the nation godly leadership when they desperately needed a fresh move of God, and this is the call that we must answer in our own nation and times.

Then the LORD came and stood and called as
at other times, "Samuel! Samuel!" And Samuel
said, "Speak, for Your servant is listening." The
LORD said to Samuel, "Behold, I am about to
do a thing in Israel at which both ears of everyone who hears it will tingle" (1 Sam. 3:10–11,
NASB).

Samuel continued as Israel's leader all the days
of his life (1 Sam. 7:15, NIV).

Spiritual barrenness is the result of neglecting or
abandoning our relationship with God. If we do not
repent, this may lead to false displays of power that will
eventually lead to disgrace. The grace we need comes
directly from God, and the acts of service we perform in
God's house will not replace spending time with Him.
Our hearts must stay close to and be available to God.
Our labor for Him and everything else we do for God
should come from hearts that are full of love for Him.

The life of Joshua, another one of Israel's leaders, is
also a powerful example of the fruits of a life that loves,
trusts, and adheres to God's word. He took over the reins
of leadership in Israel after his predecessor Moses died,
and God instructed Joshua to be obedient and meditate
on His word daily. If Joshua would give God first place in
his life, he was promised prosperity and good success in

all of his endeavors. These were God's promised blessings if he gave God his full obedience:

> Keep this Book of the Law always on your lips; meditate on it day and night, so that you may be careful to do everything written in it. Then you will be prosperous and successful (Josh. 1:8, NIV).

While Satan's disobedient and defiant ways bring destruction into our lives, loving and obeying God brings many blessings. God is the ultimate parent. Instead of experiencing evil consequences when we defy Him, He will richly bless and reward our obedience. As mentioned earlier, a rich and satisfying life is one of the many promises from God when we choose to wholeheartedly love and obey Him. "The thief's purpose is to steal and kill and destroy. My purpose is to give them a rich and satisfying life" (John 10:10, NLT).

God is also the consummate lover. He will naturally give back more than He ever receives. The highest and best blessings come from Him. We know that receiving rewards from our magnanimous Creator is not the right motive for giving Him mega love, but we simply cannot outlove or outgive God! He desires to give to us more than we could ever give to Him, and no other love can surpass His. Great fruit is produced in the lives of those who love God, and we love Him not so that we can get more out of Him—which would be exploiting His love—but because this is our joyful duty as His loving children. God has not moved from His place; we are the ones who need to return to Him. Lives are slipping away into an eternity without God, and we once again need true and fervent worshippers to be effective witnesses of God's grace.

Does your life communicate the message of God's grace effectively?

24

Job's Unsurpassable Lesson on Giving God Ultimate Love

We will end our discussion of giving God ultimate or over-the-top, mega love by learning some final lessons from a man named Job, who was the wealthiest man in his region and times. He loved God and regularly presented offerings and sacrifices to Him. His actions and holy lifestyle demonstrated that he was a true worshipper, and his family and community were all richly blessed because of Job. He was also a faithful husband and devoted father who ensured that his children did not offend God in any way. Job regularly presented special sacrifices to God on their behalf. This man, as they say, had it made. Job's impeccable character was attested to by no less than God Himself, and the blessing of God was clearly upon Job's life.

There once was a man named Job who lived
in the land of Uz. He was blameless—a man
of complete integrity. He feared God and
stayed away from evil. He had seven sons and
three daughters. He owned 7,000 sheep, 3,000
camels, 500 teams of oxen, and 500 female donkeys. He also had many servants. He was, in
fact, the richest person in that entire area" (Job
1:1–2, NLT).

"His sons used to hold feasts in their homes
on their birthdays, and they would invite their
three sisters to eat and drink with them. When
a period of feasting had run its course, Job
would make arrangements for them to be puri-
fied. Early in the morning he would sacrifice a
burnt offering for each of them, thinking, "Perhaps my children have sinned and cursed God
in their hearts." This was Job's regular custom
(Job 1:4–5, NIV).

Some have wondered whether Job was a fictional
character in the Bible, but both the prophet Ezekiel and
James, the brother of Jesus, mention him as a real histori-
cal person.

"Son of man, if a country sins against Me by
committing unfaithfulness, and I stretch out

My hand against it, destroy its supply of bread, send famine against it and cut off from it both man and beast, even though these three men, Noah, Daniel and Job were in its midst, by their own righteousness they could only deliver themselves," declares the Lord GOD . . . Or if I should send a plague against that country and pour out My wrath in blood on it to cut off man and beast from it, even though Noah, Daniel and Job were in its midst, as I live," declares the Lord GOD, "they could not deliver either their son or their daughter. They would deliver only themselves by their righteousness (Ezek. 14:13–14, 19–20 NASB).

We give great honor to those who endure under suffering. For instance, you know about Job, a man of great endurance. You can see how the Lord was kind to him at the end, for the Lord is full of tenderness and mercy (James 5:11, NLT).

With health, wealth, a thriving family, and the respect of his community, Job lacked nothing. He possessed everything a man could desire but, as was the case with Adam and Eve, God's enemy and the enemy of all that is good would soon attack Job. He would have to endure a level of suffering that would be unimaginable to most of us.

One day when Job's sons and daughters were
feasting at the oldest brother's house, a messenger arrived at Job's home with this news:
"Your oxen were plowing, with the donkeys
feeding beside them, when the Sabeans raided
us. They stole all the animals and killed all the
farmhands. I am the only one who escaped to
tell you." While he was still speaking, another
messenger arrived with this news: "The fire of
God has fallen from heaven and burned up
your sheep and all the shepherds. I am the only
one who escaped to tell you." While he was
still speaking, a third messenger arrived with
this news: "Three bands of Chaldean raiders
have stolen your camels and killed your servants. I am the only one who escaped to tell
you." While he was still speaking, another messenger arrived with this news: "Your sons and
daughters were feasting in their oldest brother's
home. Suddenly, a powerful wind swept in from
the wilderness and hit the house on all sides.
The house collapsed, and all your children are
dead. I am the only one who escaped to tell you"
(Job 1:13–19, NLT).

After he suffered these crushing losses, Job's wife,
whom he had loved so dearly, told him to just curse God
and die! She should have been the person Job could count

on. And if all this were not enough to destroy a man, his closest friends, whom he had been with for many years, also gathered around, but instead of comforting Job, they began to make false accusations against him. The destruction of everything Job possessed, compounded by the loss of his ten children, all happening within one single day, would be enough to break anyone of any stature. Such evil events after a life of faithfully serving God would be more than enough reason for anyone to stop believing in God. More dark days of satanic assaults would also follow, and what we are about to witness is the outstanding response of a true worshipper to life's worst circumstances.

Job stood up and tore his robe in grief. Then he shaved his head and fell to the ground to worship. He said, "I came naked from my mother's womb, and I will be naked when I leave. The Lord gave me what I had, and the Lord has taken it away. Praise the name of the Lord!" In all of this, Job did not sin by blaming God (Job 1:20–22, NLT).

Job was unwavering in his commitment to God in the midst of this tremendous despair. He did not permit any of these evil attacks to make a dent in his faith. Job clearly stated his heart's response to God in the following verse: "Though he slay me, yet will I hope in him;

I will surely defend my ways to his face" (Job 13:15, NIV). Distinguishing himself as a true lover of God, Job remained true to God when most of us would already be blaming God and asking Him why.

Having lost everything, Job surrendered himself to God in extreme and worshipful submission. His faith in God was inextinguishable despite the loss of all of his ten children, his assets, and even his health.

Being true to His own character and nature, God responded to Job in the same way He had with Abraham, Zechariah and Elizabeth, and many other believers when they were perplexed when it seemed that He did not care for them. First, He had great compassion for Job. Patiently and lovingly, God walked with him through this deep and dark valley of disaster and death. Some valuable lessons about handling negative experiences can be learned from Job. He went through hell and experienced some fiercely intense and painful emotions. But he only gave full vent to them in God's presence. Job met with and endured enormous challenges and unquantifiable sufferings, but he just did not let go of his faith in God.

It is impossible for us to ever fully comprehend the agonies Job went through, but his grief was palpable through his dark, emotional statements to God while he withstood his terrible ordeal. Job kept the line of communication between himself and God open, and by so doing was able to withstand the relentless slew of satanic assaults in a safe place: *God's presence*. While his feelings ranged from rage to despair, grief to anger, and unimaginable levels of depression, Job fell to the ground and still worshipped God.

After losing almost everyone dear to his heart and everything he owned, Job left us an unsurpassable lesson on giving God ultimate love.

He showed us how to handle the most difficult and unimaginable distress through worship. Job fully expressed all his negative feelings and continued to hold onto his faith throughout the intensely fierce conversations he had with God. Job let everything within him come out freely before his Creator and maker. Throughout this entire ordeal, Job conversed freely with his heavenly Father, although everyone he trusted had now abandoned him. Despite the great pain he was in, he did not hold back his innermost thoughts or bottle them up. He unloaded it all on God.

> My spirit is broken,
>> my days are cut short,
>> the grave awaits me.
> Surely mockers surround me;
>> my eyes must dwell on their hostility.
> Give me, O God, the pledge you demand.
>> Who else will put up security for me?
> You have closed their minds to understanding;
>> therefore you will not let them triumph.

If anyone denounces their friends for reward,
　　the eyes of their children will fail.
God has made me a byword to everyone,
　　a man in whose face people spit.
My eyes have grown dim with grief;
　　my whole frame is but a shadow.
The upright are appalled at this;
　　the innocent are aroused against the ungodly.
Nevertheless, the righteous will hold to their ways,
and those with clean hands will grow stronger
(Job 17:1–9, NIV).

God was not angry with or offended by Job's sincerity. He responded to his anguish with patience and great compassion. During the severe questioning that ensued between them, God answered all of Job's questions, and a rapid flurry of words was also flung at God by Job's wife and closest friends. The Lord answered all these questions with loving kindness. After the horrible ordeal was over, God comforted, replenished, and fully restored Job to wholeness. We learn from all these things that even in our darkest moments we must address our concerns and emotions in spiritually healthy ways. And the safest place to hide during the most dreadful storms in life is in God Himself: "The name of the LORD is a strong tower; the righteous man runs into it and is safe" (Prov. 18:10, ESV).

Cast your burden on the LORD, and he will sustain you; he will never permit the righteous to be moved (Ps 55:22, ESV).

Cast all your anxiety on him because he cares for you (1 Pet. 5:7, NIV).

God completely reversed Job's afflictions and restored his fortunes after his enormous struggle with Satan. He blessed Job with ten more children and doubled everything he had previously owned. We were already given the privilege earlier of knowing that Job had taught his first ten children to have faith in God and love Him. So we can safely surmise that after Job's earthly life was over, he enjoyed a joyful reunion with them in heaven. This brings Job to a grand total of twenty children, double the number he had before.

Job received double the rewards from God for everything he had lost, and his great love for God serves as one of the greatest examples of ultimate trust in Him.

After Job had prayed for his friends, the LORD restored his fortunes and gave him twice as much as he had before (Job 42:10, NIV). So the LORD blessed Job in the second half of his life even more than in the beginning. For now he had 14,000 sheep, 6,000 camels, 1,000 teams of oxen, and 1,000 female donkeys. He also gave Job seven more sons and three more daughters .... In all the land no women were as lovely as the daughters of Job. And their father put them into his will along with their brothers. Job lived 140 years after that, living to see four generations of his children and grandchildren (Job 42:12–13, 15–16, NLT).

Praise be to the Lord!

Instead of your shame you will receive a double portion, and instead of disgrace you will rejoice in your inheritance. And so you will inherit a double portion in your land, and everlasting joy will be yours (Isa. 61:7, NIV).

Unfailing love surrounds those who trust the LORD. So rejoice in the LORD and be glad, all you who obey him! Shout for joy, all you whose hearts are pure! (Ps. 32:10–11, NLT).

In the midst of life's most excruciating trials, Job surrendered his life to God in sacrificial and uncommon worship. God did not fail him. By yielding himself to God in worshipful submission, Job was able to hold onto and affirm his faith despite going through the severest trials. His life story might have taken us only a few minutes to read, but it was a long, drawn-out, and dreadful ordeal for this dear man. There are too many lessons to be drawn from Job's life for us to cover here. But here are a few more in the form of questions we can ask ourselves.

- How was Job able to endure and respond to such unexpected disaster with spontaneous worship?

- How do I build my own faith in God to remain rock-solid if I am suddenly confronted with unmitigated and unexpected hardships?

- How should a true worshipper respond to God when faced with adverse life circumstances?

- Job's life exemplifies what the motto of a true lover of God must be: In God we completely trust!

Will you place your full trust in God no matter what and give Him your over-the-top, mega love?

CPSIA information can be obtained
at www.ICGtesting.com
Printed in the USA
FSHW010457180321
79614FS